BrightRED Study Guide

Curriculum for Excellence

N5

HEALTH AND FOOD TECHNOLOGY

Janice Rodger and Pam Thomas

First published in 2013 by:
Bright Red Publishing Ltd
1 Torphichen Street
Edinburgh
EH3 8HX

A CIP record for this book is available from the British Library

ISBN 978-1-906736-39-2

With thanks to:
PDQ Digital Media Solutions Ltd (layout), Ivor Normand (copy-edit and proof-read)

Cover design and series book design by Caleb Rutherford – eidetic

Acknowledgements
Every effort has been made to seek all copyright-holders. If any have been overlooked, then Bright Red Publishing will be delighted to make the necessary arrangements.

Permission has been sought from all relevant copyright holders and Bright Red Publishing are grateful for the use of the following:

The Eatwell Plate © Crown Copyright/Department of Health in association with the Welsh Assembly Government, the Scottish Government and the Food Standards Agency in Northern Ireland (p 6 & 7); A front of pack nutrition label © Food Standards Agency (p 9); Foodpictures/Shutterstock.com (p 10); bonchan/Shutterstock.com (p 11); samoshkin/Shutterstock.com (p 11); Africa Studio/Shutterstock.com (p 13); Logo © Food Standards Agency (p 13); Africa Studio/Shutterstock.com (p 14); Douglas Freer/Shutterstock.com (p 14); Gayvoronskaya_Yana/Shutterstock.com (p 14); AN NGUYEN/Shutterstock.com (p 15); StefanoT/Shutterstock.com (p 15); Ami Parikh/Shutterstock.com (p 15); tamsindove/Shutterstock.com (p 18); Elena Elisseeva/Shutterstock.com (p 20); Robyn Mackenzie/Shutterstock.com (p 21); NataliTerr/Shutterstock.com (p 21); Elena Schweitzer/Shutterstock.com (p 21); Figure from *Food and Nutrition* by Anita Tull (3e, OUP, 1997), copyright © Oxford University Press 1983, reprinted by permission of Oxford University Press (p 23); filmfoto/Shutterstock.com (p 26); Monkey Business Images/Shutterstock.com (p 27); Dmitry Lobanov/Shutterstock.com (p 28); Designua/Shutterstock.com (p 28); Elena Stepanova/Shutterstock.com (p 30); SvetlanaFedoseyeva/Shutterstock.com (p 31); ffolas/Shutterstock.com (p 31); fasphotographic/Shutterstock.com (p 32); Poznyakov/Shutterstock.com (p 32); DoctorKan/Shutterstock.com (p 33); Pojoslaw/Shutterstock.com (p 34); Logo © The Vegetarian Society of the United Kingdom Ltd (www.vegsoc.org) (p 35); Logo © The Vegan Society (p 35); SOMMAI/Shutterstock.com (p 38); Aleksandrs Samuilovs/Shutterstock.com (p 38); Ekaterina Glazova/Shutterstock.com (p 39); phloen/Shutterstock.com (p 40); Foodpictures/Shutterstock.com (p 40); Matthew Cole/Shutterstock.com (p 42); Chad McDermott/Shutterstock.com (p 44); margouillat photo/Shutterstock.com (p 47); Eat Super Ltd (p 47); nrt/Shutterstock.com (p 49); An article taken from http://news.bbc.co.uk/1/hi/uk/828847.stm © BBC (p 49); Logo © Marine Stewardship Council (p 53); ChameleonsEye/Shutterstock.com (p 57); Logo © The Fairtrade Foundation (p 59); Logo © The Carbon Trust (p 60); Aletia/Shutterstock.com (p 60); WFP/Stephanie Savariaud (p 61); Logo © Soil Association (p 62); SasPartout/Shutterstock.com (p 63); Recycling symbol (public domain) (p 63); The advert for 'Soldiering on' © British Egg Industry Council (p 65); Verdateo/Shutterstock.com (p 68); Valentyn Volkov/Shutterstock.com (p 70); Luiz Rocha/Shutterstock.com (p 71); The article 'Menu for a ripe old age' taken from Daily Mail 20/10/2008 © Associated Newspapers Limited (p 71); Radura logo © R.M. Ulman (p 72); saddako/Shutterstock.com (p 72); saddako/Shutterstock.com (p 73); Lakeland Dairies Co-operative Society Ltd (p 75); Logo © Which? The copyright in this material is owned by Which? Limited and has been reproduced here with their permission. The logo must not be reproduced in whole or in part without the written permission of Which? Limited (p 77); Logo © Citizens Advice Scotland (p 77); FSA logo © Food Standards Agency Scotland (p 78); CookSafe logo © Food Standards Agency Food Standards Agency Scotland (p 79); A food label adapted from http://www.tradingstandards.gov.uk © Gloucestershire County Council (p 80); Pam Thomas/Ridgwell Press Ltd (p 83); Toufayan Bakeries (p 83); Recycling symbols (public domain) (p 85); Aluminium Recycling Symbol © Exonie/Creative Commons. Licenced under CC BY-SA 3.0 (http://creativecommons.org/licenses/by-sa/3.0/deed.en) (p 85); ostill/Shutterstock.com (p 87); Brent Hofacker/Shutterstock.com (p 88); Pam Thomas/Ridgwell Press Ltd (p 90).

Printed and bound in the UK by Martins the Printers.

CONTENTS

INTRODUCING NATIONAL 5 HEALTH AND FOOD TECHNOLOGY

Health and Food Technology sits within the Health and Wellbeing curriculum area of Curriculum for Excellence.

Health and Food Technology focuses on the physical, chemical, nutritional, biological and sensory properties of food. The subject provides you with opportunities to study the relationship between health, nutrition, functional properties of food, lifestyle choices and consumer issues. It develops your awareness of how food choices can have a positive effect on your own health, and it will equip you with skills and knowledge that will enable you to become a lifelong informed food consumer. You're encouraged to be creative in preparing and producing food and in evaluating finished products.

This book focuses on the core content of the National 5 syllabus for Health and Food Technology. There are three mandatory units: 'Food for Health', 'Food Product Development' and 'Contemporary Food Issues'. In addition, there is a section on the course assessment, which must be passed to gain the course award.

EXTERNAL ASSESSMENT

At the end of the course, you will be assessed externally on two components:

Component 1 – assignment – 50% of total mark

Component 2 – question paper – 50% of total mark.

The purpose of the course assessment is to assess added value. It challenges you to show depth of knowledge and skills, and it allows you to apply the skills, knowledge and understanding you've learned during the course.

Assignment

The course assignment is a problem-solving, product-development-type exercise that involves you using your skills and knowledge to investigate a food or consumer issue. It has four sections:

(1) Planning	20 marks
(2) The Product	12 marks
(3) Product Testing	10 marks
(4) Reflection	8 marks.

The assignment will be set and marked by the Scottish Qualifications Authority (SQA) and will be undertaken during class time under some supervision and control.

Question paper

The purpose of the question paper is to assess your ability to apply the knowledge and understanding gained from studying the three units, via answering a series of exam questions.

There will be five questions in the paper, each worth 10 marks. The time allocated is 1 hour and 30 minutes to complete the paper. It will be marked externally by the SQA.

The questions will sample across the whole course, including:

- Nutrients: functions and sources
- Current dietary advice and links to health, including dietary diseases

contd

- Specific dietary needs of individuals and specific groups of people
- Factors affecting consumers' choice of food
- Food labelling
- Consumer organisations
- Food product development
- Functional properties of food
- Contemporary food issues and technological developments in food production.

INTERNAL ASSESSMENT

During the course, you will be assessed on a range of skills in the context of the course content. The wide range of skills tested includes:

- Knowledge and understanding of the relationships between health, food and nutrition
- Knowledge of current dietary advice and the implications this has for long-term health and wellbeing
- Knowledge and understanding of the food product development process and the effects the functional properties of nutrients have on processing/manufacturing food products
- Make informed food and consumer choices
- Develop organisational skills to make food products that meet specific needs, using safe and hygienic working practices.

COURSE CONTENT

The course has three mandatory units: 'Food for Health', 'Food Product Development' and 'Contemporary Food Issues'.

Food for Health

The aim of this unit is to build up core knowledge of nutrition that will allow you to explain the relationship between food, health and nutrition. By exploring the dietary needs of individuals at various stages of life, this knowledge can be put into practice by the development and evaluation of food products that aim to meet individual needs.

Food Product Development

The aim of this unit is to develop knowledge and understanding of the functional properties of ingredients found in food and of their uses in developing new food products. You will be given the opportunity to work through a range of different product development briefs that will allow you to produce new food products that meet specified needs.

Contemporary Food Issues

The aim of this unit is to develop an in-depth understanding of a range of factors that affect consumers' food choices. You will consider technological developments in food manufacturing and organisations which protect consumer interests. You will also develop knowledge and understanding of food packaging, labelling and how these help consumers to make informed food choices.

This book has been developed using an interactive, contemporary approach which acknowledges the fast-paced technological society in which we are living. The broad range of activities and visual appeal throughout the book has been devised to offer lots of choice for both you and your teacher – appealing to a range of abilities and learning styles for classes while also being an effective tool for independent study.

 ONLINE

This book is supported by the BrightRED Digital Zone. Visit www.brightredbooks. net/N5HFT and log on to unlock a world of tests, games, videos and more!

FOOD FOR HEALTH

BENEFITS TO HEALTH OF A BALANCED AND VARIED DIET

DON'T FORGET

A diet isn't just about someone slimming – everyone follows a diet, as the food we eat or drink is called our 'diet'.

DON'T FORGET

The energy from what we consume is known as our energy input. The energy burned off by everyday activities is called output. You have to balance input with output to maintain a healthy weight. This is called the energy balance.

ONLINE

Undertake the Energy tutorial at www. brightredbooks.net/N5HFT. If you are confident, why not try the extension activity?

ONLINE TEST

Take the 'Benefits to Health of a Balanced and Varied Diet' test online at www. brightredbooks.net/N5HFT

VIDEO LINK

The podcast by the British Nutrition Foundation explains the Eatwell plate in a bit more detail: www. brightredbooks.net/N5HFT

WHAT IS A BALANCED DIET?

This topic is all about developing knowledge and understanding of the concept of a balanced and varied diet and its relationship to health.

There are no single foods which give the body all the nutrients it needs to be healthy and to function efficiently. Different foods give us different nutrients, so a healthy diet should contain a variety of foods to ensure that all the main nutrients are taken in. Some people may have to follow a special diet for medical or health reasons. This is covered in more detail later in this unit.

A balanced diet consists of a variety of foods which contain all the essential nutrients in the correct amount.

It also gives us the right amount of water and dietary fibre.

THE EATWELL PLATE

The Food Standards Agency has devised a pictorial guide to eating a balanced and varied diet.

This shows us our diet/the food we eat as a big plate. It tells us how we can choose a variety of foods from five different groupings of food on the plate to get the balance right.

We are encouraged to eat MORE of the foods in the larger sections of the plate (fruits and vegetables; bread, rice, potatoes, pasta and other starchy foods) and LESS of the foods in the smaller sections (meat, fish, eggs, pulses and other non-dairy sources of protein; milk and dairy foods). From the smallest section, we should try to eat least of all (food and drinks high in fat and/or sugar; also salty foods).

To maintain a healthy diet, the Eatwell plate shows you how much of what you eat should come from each food group:

The eatwell plate

Use the eatwell plate to help you get the balance right. It shows how much of what you eat should come from each food group.

Fruit and vegetables

Bread, rice, potatoes, pasta and other starchy foods

Meat, fish, eggs, pulses and other non-dairy sources of protein

Foods and drinks high in fat and/or sugar

Milk and dairy foods

BENEFITS TO HEALTH OF FOLLOWING THE ADVICE GIVEN BY THE EATWELL PLATE

Section 1 – Fruit and vegetables

- Almost all are fat-free therefore help to prevent obesity

- They are low in energy

- They provide a good source of NSP (non-starch polysaccharide, i.e. fibre), which helps to prevent bowel disorders

- They contain the antioxidant vitamins A, C and E, which can help to prevent heart disease and some cancers.

Section 2 – Bread, rice, potatoes, pasta and other starchy foods

- They are low in fat

- They can be a good source of NSP (fibre) if wholemeal or wholegrain varieties are eaten

- They contain B group vitamins

- They are a good source of slow-release energy and fill us up, so they help to prevent snacking on high-fat, high-sugar snacks and therefore can help to prevent obesity

- They contain minerals such as calcium and iron – in particular, bread is fortified with them.

Section 3 – Milk and dairy foods

- Good source of calcium, which helps with the development and maintenance of strong bones and teeth and helps to prevent osteoporosis and rickets

- They provide protein for the growth, repair and maintenance of body cells

- They provide the fat-soluble vitamins A and D and also vitamin B12.

Section 4 – Meat, fish, eggs, pulses and other non-dairy sources of protein

- All of these foods are good sources of protein for the growth, repair and maintenance of all body cells

- White fish and pulses are low in fat

- Meat is a rich source of iron, which helps to prevent anaemia

- Oily fish are a good source of essential fatty acid Omega 3, which helps to reduce the risk of heart disease

- Oily fish are also a good source of the fat-soluble vitamins A and D

- Pulses are high in fibre and contain iron.

Section 5 – Food and drinks high in fat and/or sugar

- Polyunsaturated fats such as olive oil contain essential fatty acid Omega 3, which helps to reduce the risk of heart disease

- By law, margarines are fortified with vitamins A and D.

THINGS TO DO AND THINK ABOUT

1 Undertake some research to find out more about the following terms: malnutrition, under-nutrition, Glycaemic Index (GI), Basal Metabolic Rate (BMR), legumes.

2 Create a dish that has ingredients that sample across the different food groups of the Eatwell plate.

For more activites on the benefits to health of a balanced and varied diet, turn to page 92.

ONLINE

Why not try the healthy-eating self-assessment tool to find out just how much you really know about healthy eating? www.brightredbooks.net/N5HFT

CURRENT DIETARY ADVICE

Over the years, Scotland has gained the reputation of being the 'sick man of Europe'.

This reputation has been gained because a higher percentage of the population in Scotland suffers from dietary diseases such as coronary heart disease and obesity than in most other countries in Europe.

As a result, the Scottish Dietary Targets were established as part of a diet action plan for Scotland to help the population to improve their eating habits. These targets were first published in 1996 and have since been reaffirmed in the National Food and Drink Policy.

ONLINE

Find out more about the background and the follow-up policy produced by the Scottish Government in relation to Scotland's health: www.brightredbooks.net/N5HFT

SCOTTISH DIETARY TARGETS

This table shows the **Scottish Dietary Targets**, which are the Scottish Government's preferred way of delivering current dietary advice. Of course there are also other ways, some of which we will consider later on.

You will also need to know ways to help meet these targets to help you develop healthy dishes or adapt existing ones.

Nutrient/food	Scottish Dietary Target	Ways of meeting the target
Fat	Intake of total fat should reduce to no more than 35% of total food energy.	use low-fat versions of foods such as butter or yogurt reduce intake of snacks such as crisps reduce intake of takeaway or ready meals, as these are often high in fat
Saturated fat	Average intake of saturated fat to be no more than 11% of total food energy.	use cooking methods that reduce fat content, e.g. grilling choose leaner cuts of meat, and trim visible fat from meat
Total complex carbohydrates	Increase average non-sugar carbohydrates intake by 25% through increased consumption of fruit and vegetables, bread, breakfast cereals, rice and pasta and through an increase of 25% in potato consumption.	use wholemeal varieties of products instead of white, e.g. pasta, rice, flour add pulses, pasta and rice to soups use wholegrain varieties of breakfast cereals in place of sugar-coated varieties replace chips with baked potato, rice or pasta
Sugar	Average intake of non-milk extrinsic (NME) sugars in adults not to increase. Average intake of NME sugars in children to reduce by half, i.e. to less than 10% of total energy.	replace sweet snacks, biscuits and cakes with fresh fruit drink sugar-free varieties of juices or water use artificial sweeteners in baking where appropriate replace canned fruit in syrup with canned fruit in natural juice or spring water
Salt	Average intake to reduce from 163 mmol per day to 100 mmol per day, or no more than 6g per day.	do not add salt to foods at the table taste food before adding salt use herbs and spices to flavour food avoid savoury snacks always check the label for salt content, and choose a lower variety use less salt when cooking
Fruit and vegetables	Intake to double to 400g per day. This is approximately 5 portions per day.	eat fruit and vegetables raw (e.g. carrot sticks) as snacks in place of high-fat, high-sugar snacks use fruit and vegetables in drinks, such as fresh juice or smoothies add fresh/dried fruit to breakfast cereals and yogurt add vegetables to stews, soups, curries and pizza toppings have a side of vegetables/salad with evening meal
Fish	Intake of white fish to be maintained. Intake of oily fish to double from 44g to 88g per week.	replace meat with fish for a main meal include fish as filling in sandwiches use fish in dishes such as pizza, curries and stir fry

contd

| Bread | Intake to increase by 45% from present average daily intake, mainly wholemeal and brown bread. This is approximately 6 slices per day. | eat a wider selection of breads with meals, e.g. ciabatta have a bread-based meal for lunch, e.g. a filled panini/wrap use wholemeal breadcrumbs when coating food or as a filler, e.g. in burgers replace white bread with wholemeal in sandwiches and rolls |
| Breakfast cereals | Intake to double to 34g per day. This is roughly equal to one bowl per day. | eat a bowl of a wholegrain variety for breakfast or as a snack use crushed breakfast cereals as a coating for food, or add to biscuit or scone dough |

Breast-feeding

The last Scottish Dietary Target to consider is breast-feeding. The target is that the proportion of mothers breast-feeding their babies for the first six weeks of life should increase to more than 50% from the present level, which is around 30%.

ADAPTING THE FOOD WE EAT TO HELP MEET THE SCOTTISH DIETARY TARGETS

Some of the foods we eat every day can be easily adapted to make it easier for us to try to achieve these targets.

Food	Adaptation	Reason why
white bread/flour/pasta/rice	wholemeal or wholegrain	adds fibre (NSP) to the diet
whole milk	skimmed/semi-skimmed milk	reduces saturated fat content
butter/margarine	lower-fat spread/polyunsaturated margarine	reduces saturated fat and cholesterol content of the diet
savoury snacks, e.g. crisps	low-fat varieties, e.g. baked crisps, piece of fruit	reduces fat and salt content of the diet while increasing fruit content, so helping to meet the target
sugary/fizzy drink	water, semi-skimmed milk, fresh fruit juice	reduces sugar content of the diet
biscuits/cakes	piece of fruit	helps to reduce the sugar and fat content of the diet while increasing the fruit intake

GUIDELINE DAILY AMOUNTS

To help consumers to achieve a balanced diet, the UK government has collaborated with the food industry and consumer organisations to develop a Nutrition Facts information label to go onto food products. This is the Guideline Daily Amounts label.

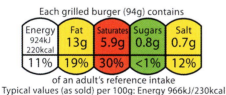

Each grilled burger (94g) contains

Energy 924kJ 220kcal	Fat 13g	Saturates 5.9g	Sugars 0.8g	Salt 0.7g
11%	19%	30%	<1%	12%

of an adult's reference intake
Typical values (as sold) per 100g: Energy 966kJ/230kcal

Guideline Daily Amounts (GDAs) provide guidelines about the approximate amounts of calories/fat/salt/sugar in a serving of food, with the aim of helping consumers to make good food choices.

THINGS TO DO AND THINK ABOUT

Choose a sweet and/or a savoury recipe you have made in school. Substitute as many ingredients as you can to make the dish(es) comply with the Scottish Dietary Targets.

Carry out a sensory testing to find out if the dishes are acceptable. Display your findings in a short report.

ONLINE TEST

Take the 'Current Dietary Advice' test online at www.brightredbooks.net/N5HFT

DON'T FORGET

For assessment purposes, it's always a good idea if you can provide specific detail when answering a question relating to current dietary advice. It's not enough at National 5 level to state something like 'eat more'.

MEETING CURRENT DIETARY ADVICE

AMENDING RECIPES TO HELP MEET CURRENT DIETARY ADVICE

As we can see from the previous page, it is fairly easy to amend our diet to help meet dietary advice. The ingredients in recipes can also be altered to make healthier versions of well-loved meals so that flavour is not lost and people are encouraged to continue eating healthily.

There are several ways this can be done:

1   By substituting ingredients for healthier ones, e.g. use skimmed milk and low-fat cheese to make a cheese sauce for use with fish or pasta, or use low-fat spread in pastry.

2   By lowering the fat, sugar and salt content of a recipe, e.g. use less oil when stir-frying vegetables (a non-stick pan needs less oil), or make good use of flavourings such as spices and herbs to cut down the need for salt or sugar.

METHODS OF COOKING FOOD TO HELP MEET CURRENT DIETARY ADVICE

Some of the foods we choose to eat are perfectly acceptable within a balanced diet; however, we do need to be careful when choosing the method of cooking these foods. This is because some methods of cooking will increase the amount of fat in the food or will cause nutrients such as vitamin C to be lost.

Grilling

Food is cooked under the direct heat of a grill or by contact with the heated elements of a grilling machine. Grilling helps meet current dietary advice because:

- the fat in the food will melt and drip out to the tray/grill pan below
- no extra fat is added to the food during cooking
- it is usually a very quick method of cooking.

Steaming

Food is cooked in the steam rising from boiling water. This can be simply by using a plate/metal steamer on top of a pan or an electric steamer specifically for this purpose. Steaming helps meet current dietary advice because:

- no salt/fat is added to the food during cooking
- food does not come into direct contact with the water, so few vitamins are lost.

Poaching

Food is covered in the minimum amount of liquid (e.g. milk, water, fruit juice) and cooked gently. Poaching helps meet current dietary advice because:

- no salt/fat is added

contd

- some vitamins may be lost in the cooking liquid, but this may be served with the food, e.g. as a sauce, so loss is lowered
- minimum cooking time and amount of liquid also help to reduce loss of vitamins.

Stir-frying

Vegetables, chicken, fish and meat can be sliced thinly and stirred quickly in a small amount of hot oil for a very short time. Stir-frying helps meet current dietary advice because:

- only a small amount of oil is used
- food is cooked quickly, so nutrient loss is minimal.

Microwaving

Food is cooked by the penetrating electromagnetic waves of a microwave oven. Food is cooked very quickly, as the waves cause the food to be heated from the inside to the outside. Microwaving helps meet current dietary advice because:

- no fat needs to be added
- food is cooked quickly, so few nutrients are lost
- no salt is added to the food.

Pressure cooking

This is a method of cooking where the boiling point of water is increased using a special sealed pan, causing the food to cook faster – up to 10 times. Pressure cooking helps meet current dietary advice because:

- food is cooked quickly, so few nutrients – especially vitamins – are lost.

Temperature
Tight-fitting lid prevents steam from escaping and allows temperature to exceed 100°C

steam
121°C

Safety
Handle locks lid shut and cannot be opened when pot is under pressure

Heat
Moist steam atmosphere is in direct contact with surface of food which allows it to cook very quickly

Pressure
Steam is released here to keep pressure stable inside pot – up to 15 pounds per square inch

 ONLINE

Check out the link 'NHS: Eat Less Saturated Fat' to read more about how to reduce fat intake: www.brightredbooks.net/N5HFT

 ONLINE TEST

Take the 'Meeting Scottish Dietary Targets' test online at www.brightredbooks.net/N5HFT

 DON'T FORGET

Food is cooked to make it taste better and to make it safer and easier to eat; however, it is important to remember that some nutrients change/are lost during cooking while others remain unchanged. Some methods add fat, while others will help to remove fat.

THINGS TO DO AND THINK ABOUT

Some people say they cannot eat a healthy diet because they do not have a lot of money, and fresh food can be expensive. This doesn't have to be the case. Use the information from the 'Eatwell' link at www.brightredbooks.net/N5HFT to devise a poster/leaflet/booklet that provides those on a low income with some valuable suggestions as to how to eat healthily.

MAINTAINING A HEALTHY DIET

PREPARATION TECHNIQUES FOR HEALTHY EATING

Cooking fresh vegetables can help to release certain nutrients, making them more available to the body. However, poor preparation, handling and cooking can destroy essential nutrients, especially vitamin C and folate.

Here is a list of rules to follow to help preserve these essential nutrients:

1. Storage

Store vegetables carefully – the salad-crisper section of your fridge is designed to be slightly cooler and more humid than the upper area, so is more suited to vegetable storage. The less contact fruit and vegetables have with the air, the better. Storing in a cool, dark place helps prevent oxidisation.

2. Skins

It is better for nutrient content if the skins of fruit and vegetables are left on. Not only does peeling expose the flesh to the air, but also vitamins and minerals are often found in or just under the skin and so are quickly lost. If vegetables do need to be peeled, try to do it just before use and do not soak them, as water-soluble vitamins will be lost in the water.

3. Chopping

Try to chop/slice vegetables into larger pieces. This will reduce the surface area exposed to air and so minimise nutrient loss. Some vegetables can be cooked whole, e.g. potatoes can be boiled whole in their skins and sliced or chopped after cooking.

4. Solubility

Vegetables should be cooked in the minimum amount of water possible. The water-soluble vitamins B and C will leach out into the cooking water and vanish down the drain. To avoid this, the cooking liquid could be used as the base for soup or gravy.

5. Heat

Cook vegetables for as short a time as possible – the longer the cooking time, the more vitamins are destroyed, as vitamin B complex and C are susceptible to heat. Vitamin C is particularly vulnerable to heat, as it is lost in temperatures below boiling point.

6. Alkalinity

Vitamin C is lost during cooking if bicarbonate of soda is added to the water. This is often added to cooking liquid to enhance the colour of green vegetables; however, it does destroy vitamin C, therefore it should be avoided.

7. Leftovers

Leftovers should be reheated as quickly as possible to avoid further loss of nutrients.

DON'T FORGET

When the skins are left on, remember to clean vegetables thoroughly to help prevent food poisoning.

DON'T FORGET

Steaming is a good alternative to boiling most vegetables to help minimise loss.

THE 8 TIPS FOR HEALTHY EATING

The Scottish Dietary Targets are not the only current dietary advice that is useful to follow.

The Food Standards Agency recommends that you follow the Eatwell plate (see pages 6–7) and use the 8 Tips for Healthy Eating to allow you to make better food choices.

These tips give practical advice on how to follow a healthy diet and are as follows:

1 Base meals on starchy foods

2 Eat lots of fruit and vegetables

3 Eat more fish

4 Cut down on saturated fat and sugar

5 Try to eat less salt – no more than 6g per day

6 Get active and try to be a healthy weight

7 Drink plenty of water

8 Don't skip breakfast.

THINGS TO DO AND THINK ABOUT

Find out why breakfast is considered to be important in a healthy diet.

Develop a recipe that will encourage teenagers to eat breakfast.

DON'T FORGET

Microwaving is a very quick method of cooking/reheating and may help to minimise loss of vitamins.

ONLINE

Look at the information about the 8 tips: www.brightredbooks.net/N5HFT

ONLINE

Try the '8 tips for eating well' tutorial – www.brightredbooks.net/N5HFT

ONLINE TEST

Take the 'Maintaining a Healthy Diet' test online at www.brightredbooks.net/N5HFT

FUNCTIONS AND EFFECTS ON HEALTH OF THE MAIN NUTRIENTS 1

NUTRIENTS AND THEIR FUNCTIONS AND SOURCES

As we have already seen, we need a variety of foods to give us a balanced diet. This is because different foods give us different **nutrients**.

Each nutrient has a specific function (use/job to do) in the body – and this will also affect health.

There are five main nutrient groups that you will need to study to succeed at National 5:

- Proteins – high and low biological value
- Fats – saturated and unsaturated
- Carbohydrates – sugars and starches
- Vitamins – fat-soluble and water-soluble
- Minerals – iron and calcium.

DON'T FORGET

Also important in our daily diet, although they are not nutrients, are water and dietary fibre (non-starch polysaccharide, or NSP).

PROTEINS

Proteins are made up of chains of amino acids.

There are over 20 different amino acids. Our bodies can make some of these amino acids but not all of them.

Adults need 8 of these and children need 10 for normal growth. These are called the **essential amino acids**.

Foods which contain all of the 10 essential amino acids are said to be of **high biological value** and are mainly found in foods from animal sources – the main exception being soya beans.

Foods which lack at least one essential amino acid are said to be of **low biological value**. These are mainly from plant sources such as beans and lentils.

VIDEO LINK

Watch the video links 'The role of protein' and 'Pointers on protein' at www.brightredbooks.net/N5HFT for more information on the role of protein in the diet.

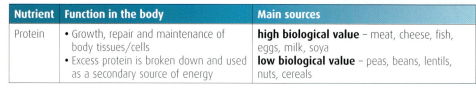

Nutrient	Function in the body	Main sources
Protein	• Growth, repair and maintenance of body tissues/cells • Excess protein is broken down and used as a secondary source of energy	**high biological value** – meat, cheese, fish, eggs, milk, soya **low biological value** – peas, beans, lentils, nuts, cereals

FATS

Fats can be classified as either **saturated** or **unsaturated**.

Saturated fats

These mainly come from animal sources such as butter and lard. The two exceptions are palm oil and coconut oil.

These are generally considered to be bad for our health, as they could increase the risk of coronary heart disease.

contd

Unsaturated fats

These mainly come from plant sources and can be split into two groups:

- **Monounsaturated fats**, which include olive oil and fish oils
- **Polyunsaturated fats**, which include certain types of margarine and sunflower oil.

These are generally considered to be better for healh than saturated fats and have been shown to help reduce blood cholesterol, which means there is less risk of coronary heart disease.

Essential fatty acids are found in unsaturated fats. They have to be found in food, as the body cannot manufacture them itself.

Nutrient	Function in the body	Main sources
Fats	• Concentrated source of energy • Warmth – excess fats consumed and not used for energy are converted to body fat and stored under the skin, providing a layer of insulation • Source of the fat-soluble vitamins A, D, E and K	**Saturates:** cream, butter, lard, suet, dripping, meat, full-cream milk **Unsaturates:** Mono – olive oil, fish oils, avocado Poly – sunflower oil, corn oil

DON'T FORGET

Essential Fatty Acids = Omega 3 and Omega 6

VIDEO LINK

The clip 'Fats in our diet' gives an explanation of this: www.brightredbooks.net/N5HFT

CARBOHYDRATES

Carbohydrates can be divided into three main groups:

- **Monosaccharides**
- **Disaccharides**
- **Polysaccharides.**

Monosaccharides and disaccharides are also known as sugars.

Polysaccharides are also known as starches or total complex carbohydrates (TCC).

Nutrient	Function in the body	Main sources
Carbohydrates	• Major source of **energy** for all body activities • **Warmth** – excess carbohydrates consumed and not used for energy are converted to body fat and stored under the skin, providing a layer of insulation	**Sugars**: fruit and vegetables, refined sugar, sweets, jams, soft drinks **Starches**: cereals, e.g. wheat, oats, rice; cereal products, e.g. bread, pasta, potatoes, lentils

VIDEO LINK

You should check out the clip 'Carbohydrate and fibre' for more information at www.brightredbooks.net/N5HFT

THINGS TO DO AND THINK ABOUT

Click on the link at www.brightredbooks.net/N5HFT to work through the interactive macronutrients tutorial.

Or make and reflect on a high-protein, low-carbohydrate food product suitable for a vegetarian.

ONLINE TEST

Take the 'Functions and Effects on Health of the Main Nutrients: Proteins, Fats and Carbohydrates' test online at www.brightredbooks.net/N5HFT

FUNCTIONS AND EFFECTS ON HEALTH OF THE MAIN NUTRIENTS 2

VITAMINS: AN INTRODUCTION

Vitamins are essential for the general health of the body. They are only needed in very small amounts.

Most vitamins cannot be made in the body, so need to be found in our diet.

Vitamins are classified as either fat-soluble or water-soluble.

FAT-SOLUBLE VITAMINS

The fat-soluble vitamins are A, D, E and K. These are transported around your body in fat cells and need fat to be absorbed. If your diet contains more of these vitamins than required at any one time, they can be stored in your fat and liver cells.

Nutrient	Function in the body	Main sources
Vitamin A	• Needed for growth in children • Assists with good eyesight, particularly in dim light • Normal function and structure of the skin and mucous membranes • Helps with resistance to infection • Classed as an **antioxidant vitamin**	**Animal sources**: liver, whole milk, cheese, butter, margarine, sardines, fish oils, meat **Plant sources**: dark green leafy vegetables, carrots, orange-coloured fruits, e.g. mango
Vitamin D	• Assists with the absorption of calcium and phosphorus • Assists calcium and phosphorus with the development and maintenance of strong bones and teeth • Helps bone fractures to heal more quickly • Is needed for the clotting of blood	The main source of vitamin D is sunlight Egg yolk, fish liver oils, liver, oily fish, margarine **Fortified** breakfast cereals
Vitamin E	• Helps to maintain cell membranes • Classed as an **antioxidant vitamin**	Vegetable oils, nuts, margarine, wheat germ, oatmeal, eggs Fortified breakfast cereals
Vitamin K	• Is needed for the clotting of blood	Green leafy vegetables, milk eggs, dairy produce

WATER-SOLUBLE VITAMINS

Water-soluble vitamins include the B-group vitamins and vitamin C. They dissolve in water and cannot be stored by the body. Excess amounts are eliminated in urine, so must be replaced every day in our diet to provide a continuous supply and ensure that no deficiency occurs.

Water-soluble vitamins are also easily destroyed or washed away during food storage and preparation, but following correct procedures in these two areas can help to reduce this loss.

VITAMIN B GROUP

There are a number of different B vitamins, all of which have some features in common; however, each one has its own specific role to play as well.

Nutrient	Function in the body	Main sources
Vitamin B group	• Release of energy from food • Maintains healthy nervous system • Needed for cell reproduction • Required for normal growth in children	Offal, wholegrain products, cereals, nuts and green vegetables.
B1 (thiamine)	• Release of energy from carbohydrates • Helps with functioning of the nervous system • Helps to maintain muscle function	Beef, brewer's yeast, beans, lentils, milk, nuts, oats, oranges, pork, rice, seeds, wheat, wholegrain cereals and yeast. Foods made with white rice or white flour are often fortified with thiamine, because most of it is lost during the refinement process.
B2 (riboflavin)	• Release of energy from protein, fats and carbohydrates • Required for normal growth in children • Helps to keep skin, eyes and nervous system healthy	Milk and dairy products, fish, meat, liver, kidney, green leafy vegetables, wholegrain and fortified cereals, bread.
Folic acid/ folate	• Works together with vitamin B12 to form healthy red blood cells • Helps reduce the risk of central-nervous-system defects such as spina bifida in unborn babies	Broccoli, brussels sprouts, liver, spinach, asparagus, peas, chickpeas, brown rice, fortified breakfast cereals.

VITAMIN C

Vitamin C is also known as ascorbic acid and cannot be stored in the body, so you need it in your diet every day.

You should be able to get all the vitamin C you need from your daily diet.

Nutrient	Function in the body	Main sources
Vitamin C	• Helps protect cells and keeps them healthy • Is necessary for the maintenance of healthy connective tissue, which gives support and structure for other tissue and organs • Helps wounds to heal • Helps with the absorption of iron and so helps to prevent anaemia • Helps prevent infections • Helps cuts and wounds to heal • Classed as an **antioxidant vitamin**	Oranges, orange juice and other citrus fruits, red and green peppers, strawberries, blackcurrants, broccoli, brussels sprouts, potatoes, blueberries, mango, papaya, cantaloupe, spinach, kiwi fruit

People who drink alcohol regularly, smoke or are on a restricted diet may have an insufficient intake of vitamin C. Alcohol prevents vitamin C absorption, and cigarettes deplete vitamin C levels.

People with wounds, burns or pneumonia, or who are recovering from surgery/illness, may need more vitamin C to support the healing process.

ANTIOXIDANT VITAMINS

Vitamins A, C and E (the ACE vitamins) are antioxidants.

Antioxidants are substances that may help to protect your cells against the harmful effects of free radicals. Free radicals are manufactured by the body when breaking down food or when exposed to environmental substances such as tobacco smoke and radiation. Free radicals can damage cells and may play a role in heart disease and cancer.

THINGS TO DO AND THINK ABOUT

Use the information from the 'Free Radical' website to produce a poster that shows what free-radical cell damage is, and how you can protect against it.

ONLINE

Look at the 'Free Radical' information from the Health Defence website: www.brightredbooks.net/N5HFT.

ONLINE TEST

Take the 'Functions and Effects on Health of the Main Nutrients: Vitamins' test online at www.brightredbooks.net/N5HFT

DON'T FORGET

Free radicals are chemicals without paired electrons, therefore they steal electrons from other molecules, which causes the damage.

FUNCTIONS AND EFFECTS ON HEALTH OF THE MAIN NUTRIENTS 3

MINERALS: AN INTRODUCTION

Minerals are naturally occurring compounds that rocks are made of. They are classified as either major or trace elements.

Minerals are essential to the general health of the body – and, although each one has its own particular function, they are all important.

Some minerals are needed in larger amounts than others, e.g. calcium and phosphorus.

Others are needed in smaller amounts and are known as trace minerals, e.g. iron and fluoride.

CALCIUM

Nutrient	Function in the body	Main sources
Calcium	• Growth, development and maintenance of strong bones and teeth • Prevents **rickets** in children • Helps with the clotting of blood • Required for the normal functioning of nerves and muscles/helps muscle control	Milk, cheese, yogurt Tinned fish with edible bones, e.g. salmon/sardines Green leafy vegetables Flour, **fortified** white bread Soya beans

IRON

Nutrient	Function in the body	Main sources
Haem iron (animal sources)	Required for the formation of haemoglobin/ red blood cells	Liver Meat Seafood Poultry
Non-haem iron (vegetable sources)	Carries oxygen around the body/prevents anaemia	Green leafy vegetables Nuts Seeds Wholegrain cereals

PHOSPHORUS

Nutrient	Function in the body	Main sources
Phosphorus	• Works with calcium to give strength to bones and teeth • Helps to release energy from food	Milk and milk products Meat and meat products Cereal products, nuts, fish

SODIUM

Nutrient	Function in the body	Main sources
Sodium	• Needed to maintain the correct concentration of fluid in the body • Needed for correct muscle function • Needed for correct nerve function	Salt Bacon, cheese Savoury snacks, convenience foods, processed meats

FLUORIDE

Nutrient	Function in the body	Main sources
Fluoride	• Essential for hardening the enamel on teeth • Ensures that bones have the correct amount of minerals deposited in them	Drinking water – especially if it has been fluoridised Small amounts may be found in tea and saltwater fish

Too much fluoride in the diet can have an adverse effect on teeth and may lead to discolouring or mottling.

THINGS TO DO AND THINK ABOUT

1   Design a dish to include ingredients that are high in iron and that enhance the absorption of iron. Make sure you identify these ingredients. Produce the dish and then undertake nutritional analysis to see if your dish meets the Dietary Reference Value figure for iron for your age group/gender.

2   Draw two columns on a page – one headed 'Food', the other headed 'Nutrients'.

Write down the food you have eaten today in the food column. In the second column, work out which nutrients are in the foods you have eaten. Use a different colour of pen/highlighter for each nutrient.

Are there any missing? How could you ensure that you make this deficiency up?

Is there too much of any nutrient? Describe how this could be a problem, and suggest ways to cut down.

DON'T FORGET

A healthy person will only absorb around 10% of iron from food intake. Animal sources are more readily absorbed by the body. Foods containing vitamin C are necessary to aid the absorption of iron. A high fibre intake can decrease the absorption of iron.

DON'T FORGET

Calcium combines with phosphorus to form **calcium phosphate**.
This is the material that gives bones and teeth their hardness and is essential to help prevent dietary diseases such as **rickets** in children, **osteomalacia** and **osteoporosis**.

DON'T FORGET

Although we are recommended to cut down on the amount of sodium we have in our diet as too much may lead to high blood pressure, it is still an important mineral and has its own specific functions in the body.

DON'T FORGET

Most toothpastes on sale have fluoride added to them; however, this should not be relied upon as a good source.

ONLINE

Take the 'Nutrients in Food Quiz' at www.brightredbooks. net/N5HFT

ONLINE TEST

Take the 'Functions and Effects on Health of the Main Nutrients: Minerals' test online at www. brightredbooks.net/N5HFT

HEALTH AND NUTRIENT INTAKE

WATER

Water is essential to life. We cannot survive long without it – but it is not a nutrient.

The body is made up of around 65% water, and some is lost daily through sweat, urine, faeces and breathing, therefore we need to have a regular intake of fluids. Some reports recommend at least 8 drinks per day, including fruit juice, tea, coffee and diluted drinks.

	Function in the body	Main sources
Water	• required for all body fluids, e.g. blood • required to regulate body temperature • assists with removal of waste products • required for all bodily processes to take place, e.g. digestion • lubricates joints and mucous membranes	Drinking water Most foods contain some water; however – Fruit and vegetables consist mainly of water

Sometimes our requirement for fluids is increased:

- during exercise
- in hot weather
- during lactation (breastfeeding)
- during illness (e.g. vomiting/diarrhoea).

NSP (FIBRE)

NSP is an abbreviation for non-starch polysaccharide. It is also known as dietary fibre.

Like water, it is not classed as a nutrient. This is because it cannot be digested by the body. Instead, it passes through the digestive system, absorbing water and helping to make faeces softer and easier to push out of the body. This helps to prevent bowel disorders, which we shall cover in more detail later on.

	Function in the body	Main sources
NSP (fibre)	• A diet high in NSP can help to prevent bowel disorders such as constipation • NSP absorbs water and binds with waste products to make faeces bulky and easier to remove from the body • NSP helps to give the body a feeling of fullness which may prevent snacking on high-fat/sugary snacks, thus helping to prevent obesity • NSP helps to 'mop up' any poisonous toxins found in waste products • NSP helps to remove cholesterol from the body	Fruit (with the skin on) Vegetables, especially leafy Potato skins Wholegrain cereals Brown rice and pasta Wholemeal bread

MULTI-NUTRIENT VALUE OF FOOD

Most foods contain more than one nutrient and so are of use to the body in several ways. However, there is no single food which will provide the body with every nutrient it needs. Therefore we need a variety of foods within a balanced diet to stay healthy.

THE RELATIONSHIP BETWEEN HEALTH AND ENERGY

Energy is needed by the body to carry out all processes and activities, including breathing and sleeping.

When the body digests fats, proteins and carbohydrates, energy is released, thus allowing these activities to take place.

It is important that the amount of energy that you consume is balanced with the amount of energy you expend on processes and activities. If the intake of energy is much higher than the energy used, the excess will be stored under the skin as body fat.

contd

If the intake of energy is lower than the energy used, then the body will be tired, will lack enthusiasm for activity and may lose weight.

THE RELATIONSHIP BETWEEN HEALTH AND PROTEIN

We have seen that protein is needed by the body for the growth, repair and maintenance of cells. If too much protein is eaten in comparison to what is needed, any excess will be turned into energy. This energy is added to the intake already there and so, if not used up in activity, will be stored as body fat. Protein is said to have a high satiety value, i.e. it keeps you feeling fuller longer.

INTERRELATIONSHIP OF NUTRIENTS

While the body needs nutrients to function properly, some of them need to work together to ensure that the body stays healthy.

Iron and vitamin C

Much of the iron that we take in – particularly plant sources of iron – is not actually absorbed by the body. In fact, a healthy person only absorbs about 10% of the iron that is in the food they eat.

Vitamin C helps the body to change the iron which cannot be absorbed into a form which can be more readily used by the body.

Calcium, phosphorus and vitamin D

Calcium and phosphorus are needed by the body for the formation and maintenance of strong bones and teeth. They do this by combining to form a substance called calcium phosphate, which is the material that gives bones and teeth their hardness. This process is called **calcification**.

Vitamin D is important, as it controls the absorption of these two minerals and helps to ensure that there is enough available for the body to perform this process. If the body is lacking in vitamin D, then less calcium and phosphorus will be available to strengthen bones and teeth, which will increase the risk of deficiency diseases such as rickets.

DON'T FORGET

Sunlight is an important source of vitamin D in this country.

FACTORS HINDERING THE ABSORPTION OF NUTRIENTS

We have seen how the absorption of calcium is helped by vitamin D, and iron is assisted by vitamin C; however, the presence of some chemicals found in foods hinders or prevents these minerals from being absorbed.

Iron absorption is hindered by:

- NSP (fibre)
- phytic acid (a type of acid found in wholegrains)
- lack of vitamin C.

Calcium absorption is hindered by:

- saturated fats
- phytic acid
- oxalic acid (often found in green vegetables)
- NSP (fibre)
- lack of vitamin D.

THINGS TO DO AND THINK ABOUT

1 Choose a dish you enjoy eating, and create a mind-map to show all the nutrients it contains.

2 Design and make a main course including iron and vitamin C. If you have access to a nutrition program, run your meal through it to find out exactly how much of each is present.

ONLINE TEST

Take the 'Health and Nutrient Intake' test online at www.brightredbooks.net/N5HFT

EFFECTS OF DIET-RELATED CONDITIONS OR DISEASES ON HEALTH 1

As we have seen, a balanced diet and intake of the correct amount of nutrients helps to keep the body healthy.

Sometimes, if a diet is poor-quality or has too much or too little of any of the nutrients, or there is a generally unwise food choice, then the risk of developing illnesses and serious diet-related diseases is increased.

At National 5 level, you will be expected to explain the causes and effects on health of at least three diet-related conditions which could include the following:

- anaemia
- bowel disorders (constipation, piles, diverticulitis, bowel cancer)
- coronary heart disease
- dental caries (tooth decay)
- hypertension/high blood pressure and strokes
- obesity
- Type 2 diabetes
- osteoporosis.

Let's start by looking at anaemia and bowel disorders.

DON'T FORGET

Teenage girls are extremely susceptible to anaemia due to menstruation.

DON'T FORGET

Vitamin B12 is only found in animal sources, so vegans may be more susceptible to this disorder.

ANAEMIA

Anaemia is a condition where there is a reduced number of red blood cells or amount of haemoglobin in the blood.

There are several different types of anaemia. Each one has a different cause, although iron-deficiency anaemia is the most common type. This is when the body does not get enough iron from the diet. If the body's iron stores aren't replenished, then continuing iron deficiency can cause the body's normal haemoglobin production to slow down. When haemoglobin levels and red blood-cell production drop below normal, a person is said to have anaemia.

Other forms of anaemia can be caused by a lack of vitamin B12 or folate in the body and a low rate of iron absorption from the iron that is taken in.

red blood cells

normal   anaemic

Effects on health

The main effects of **iron-deficiency anaemia** on health are that it can cause severe tiredness and lethargy (lack of energy). The face appears pale, and the gums lack colour.

Other symptoms of this disease include breathlessness or dizziness, and sometimes a sufferer may experience a racing pulse.

Anaemia caused by **lack of vitamin B12** can cause depression and confusion, colour blindness and abnormal nervous reactions.

Anaemia caused by a **lack of folate/folic acid** can cause neural tube defects (spina bifida) in unborn babies and neurological abnormalities in children.

ONLINE

Listen to the BBC radio broadcast 'Iron Deficiency Anaemia' at www. brightredbooks.net/N5HFT. Take notes as you listen.

How it can be prevented

The risk of anaemia can be greatly reduced by ensuring that the diet contains enough iron-rich foods.

The absorption of iron can be improved by ensuring that foods containing vitamin C are included along with foods containing iron. This is because the presence of vitamin C greatly enhances the absorption of iron in the body.

BOWEL DISORDERS

The bowel is the lower part of the digestive system, also known as the colon.

A diet low in NSP (dietary fibre) and fluids can lead to several different bowel disorders, all of which have an adverse effect on health. The advice on fibre intake is to aim to consume 18g of fibre per day.

(a) High-fibre diet – the soft, large faeces are moved along the intestine easily.

(b) Low-fibre diet – the small, hard faeces cannot be moved so easily, and extra effort is required to push them.

(c) This leads to the development of diverticula.

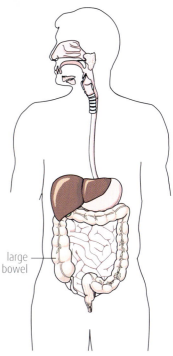

large bowel

This table lists typical symptoms and conditions related to bowel disorders:

Condition	Symptom
Constipation	Waste products (faeces) become hard, dry and slow to move through the digestive system, making them difficult to pass out. Bowel movements are infrequent, and a lot of effort is needed to remove the waste, often resulting in straining. Abdominal discomfort and a general feeling of ill health often accompany this condition.
Piles (haemorrhoids)	Piles are swellings that contain enlarged and swollen blood vessels in and around the rectum and anus. These can be caused by prolonged constipation.
Diverticular disease/ diverticulitis	These are related conditions that affect the colon. Small bulges develop on the lining of the colon and may become inflamed or infected, causing abdominal pain, cramps, bloating and excess wind. More common in the elderly who have a weakened intestine, it is also associated with long-term constipation.
Bowel cancer	Blood present in faeces and/or bleeding from the anus, prolonged bouts of constipation or diarrhoea, unexplained weight loss and abdominal pain are some of the symptoms; however, age is also a major factor, as bowel cancer is more common in the elderly.

Preventing bowel disorders

Once again, following the advice of the Eatwell plate is key to preventing bowel disorders.

Eating a diet which is low in saturated fat and high in fruit and vegetables (at least five portions per day) and high in wholegrain has been shown to greatly reduce the risk. Red- and processed-meat intake should also be kept to below 70g per day.

Lifestyle factors such as cutting down on alcohol and smoking, and increasing exercise, also lower the risk of these disorders.

THINGS TO DO AND THINK ABOUT

Develop a questionnaire (either using paper copies or an online survey tool – see pages 44-47 for methods of investigation for additional advice). The focus should be on finding out as much as you can about people's fibre intake in their daily diet and how prevalent bowel disorders are. Follow up this activity with developing a high-fibre snack. Evaluate the fibre content of your product via undertaking nutritional analysis.

ONLINE

For more information, read 'Introduction: Constipation' at www.brightredbooks.net/N5HFT

VIDEO LINK

The link 'Piles: what is it?' is a short clip with an expert explaining what piles are, who gets them and how to get rid of them: www.brightredbooks.net/N5HFT

ONLINE TEST

Take the 'Effects of diet-related conditions or diseases on health: Anaemia and Bowel Disorders' test online at www.brightredbooks.net/N5HFT

EFFECTS OF DIET-RELATED CONDITIONS OR DISEASES ON HEALTH 2

CORONARY HEART DISEASE: AN INTRODUCTION

Coronary heart disease is one of the major causes of death in Scotland and in the rest of the developed world. It costs the NHS millions of pounds a year to treat.

What happens when fatty material builds up in the arteries

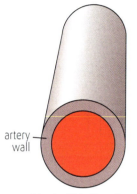  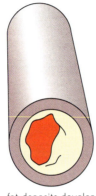

artery wall

blood within the artery

atheroma (fatty deposits) building up

fat deposits develop, restricting the blood flow through the artery

In order to function normally, the heart needs a good supply of oxygenated blood in the coronary arteries so that it can pump the blood through the vessels to the brain and other parts of the body.

Sometimes, these coronary arteries become blocked with fatty deposits. These deposits are made up mostly of a waxy substance called **cholesterol**.

Cholesterol is important in the body, as it forms cell membranes, hormones and other tissues. Cholesterol in the blood is attached to a protein molecule called a lipoprotein. However, if the level of cholesterol in the blood is too high, the risk of developing these fatty deposits is increased, and so the risk of developing coronary heart disease is high.

DON'T FORGET

The body can make all the cholesterol we need; the liver produces on average 1000mg of cholesterol each day. Some of this cholesterol is used to produce sex hormones; it has a role in producing hormones that regulate blood-sugar levels; and the body can even use cholesterol to make vitamin D when our skin is exposed to sunlight.

SYMPTOMS/EFFECT ON HEALTH

If the coronary arteries become narrow and blocked, blood carrying oxygen cannot reach the heart so easily. This causes the heart muscle to become starved of oxygen, which will induce severe cramp-like pains in the chest, left arm and neck. This will eventually die down with rest and medication but is brought on by stress, exercise and anything else which causes the heart to work harder. Someone with coronary heart disease has a low quality of life in that they are unable to do lots of everyday activities without becoming breathless and experiencing chest pains. Shopping, walking up stairs and running for a bus are very difficult indeed.

HEART ATTACK

If the blockage becomes severe and complete, then the blood will not be able to get through and may start to form a clot. The person will then suffer a heart attack. This will badly damage the heart muscle and could lead to the heart stopping completely. This is called a cardiac arrest – and, unless emergency first aid is at hand, the person will die.

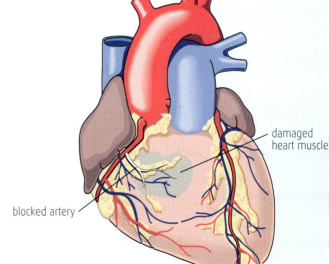

damaged heart muscle

blocked artery

ONLINE TEST

Take the 'Effects of diet-related conditions or diseases on health: Coronary Heart Disease' test online at www.brightredbooks.net/N5HFT

PREVENTING CORONARY HEART DISEASE

Coronary heart disease can be caused by problems relating to diet – if we address these problems then we can reduce the risk of developing coronary heart disease (CHD).

These diet-related problems include a diet which is high in:

- Fat – in particular saturated fat can raise cholesterol levels.
- Sugar – people who develop Type 2 diabetes are more at risk of heart disease.
- Salt – too much can lead to High Blood Pressure.
- Alcohol – a high intake may lead to High Blood Pressure.

These are also all high in energy which, if not used up, can lead to obesity.

Other diet-related problems which can lead to the development of CHD are diets low in:

- Fruit and vegetables – which contain the ACE (antioxidant) vitamins.
- Dietary Fibre (NSP) – this can help to reduce the cholesterol in the blood; it also fills us up and so may prevent snacking on sugary/fatty foods.
- Polyunsaturated Fats – these have been shown to reduce the risk of blood clots forming so lowering the risk of a heart attack. Omega 3 may help prevent the build up of cholesterol in the blood.

Coronary Heart Disease may also be caused by non-dietary factors:

- Smoking – cigarettes contain a substance called nicotine which causes the heart to beat faster so increasing the risk of high blood pressure and CHD.
- Lack of regular exercise – exercise can reduce the risk of obesity and high blood pressure.
- Age – as people get older, they may become less active.
- Heredity – there may be a greater risk of someone developing CHD if there is a history of it in the family.
- Lifestyle factors – more and more people are relying on pre-prepared, convenient food such as ready meals and take away foods which can be high in hidden fat and salt. More people also now eat snacks between meals. These snacks are often high in sugar/fat.

Therefore, to reduce the risk of coronary heart disease, we should reduce our overall intake of fat, and replace saturated fats with polyunsaturates, and reduce alcohol intake.

A diet rich in the antioxidant vitamins A, C and E will help to stop cholesterol sticking to the artery walls.

A diet high in soluble fibre can also help to remove fatty deposits from the body – remember the target is to consume at least 18g of fibre per day.

VIDEO LINK

Watch the video on the BrightRED Digital Zone to find out more about Coronary heart disease in Scotland.

VIDEO LINK

Find out more by watching the clip 'Understanding Cholesterol' at www.brightredbooks.net/N5HFT

THINGS TO DO AND THINK ABOUT

How good is your diet? Take the 'Healthy Eating self assessment' quiz at www.brightredbooks.net/N5HFT

EFFECTS OF DIET-RELATED CONDITIONS OR DISEASES ON HEALTH 3

HYPERTENSION AND STROKES

Hypertension is another name for high blood pressure.

When your heart beats, it pumps blood around your body to give you the energy and oxygen you need. As the blood moves, it pushes against the side of the blood vessels. The strength of this pushing is your blood pressure. This pressure changes according to the activity you are doing and/or how fast your heart is beating.

Blood pressure can be increased if the artery walls have thickened and have fatty deposits, causing them to narrow. A clot may form, causing the blood flow to be interrupted and the brain to be starved of oxygen.

If your blood pressure remains high for too long, strain is put on your heart and blood vessels. Over time, this increases the risk of heart disease, heart attacks and strokes.

How to lower blood pressure

One of the easiest ways to reduce blood pressure is to reduce the amount of salt in the diet. Salt makes your body retain water, which will be stored in the body, causing blood pressure to increase. So, decreasing intake to less than 6g per day should reduce blood pressure.

Tips for reducing salt in the diet include:

- Do not add salt when cooking – this includes stock cubes and soy sauce.
- Flavour foods instead with herbs and spices and seasonings like ginger, chilli and lemon juice.
- Cut down on processed and takeaway foods, which may be high in salt.
- Look for lower-salt alternatives to table sauces and breakfast cereals.
- Always check labels and compare products for the salt content.
- If you really can't do without salt, use a small amount of a low-sodium substitute.

DON'T FORGET

Other factors include obesity, lack of exercise and high alcohol intake. Risk of high blood pressure also increases with age.

VIDEO LINK

Look at the clip about strokes and the 'FAST' way of dealing with an emergency: www.brightredbooks.net/N5HFT

DENTAL CARIES

Dental caries is also known as dental or tooth decay. This happens when acids in your mouth dissolve the outer layers of your teeth (enamel).

Symptoms

Symptoms of tooth decay include:

- Toothache
- Pain when eating and drinking
- Visible spots and marks on teeth.

If left untreated, a build-up of a sticky substance on the teeth, called plaque, could lead to gum disease and abscesses and eventually loss of teeth completely. Plaque is a combination of food particles and bacteria. If the plaque isn't removed, the bacteria break it down, and acid is formed.

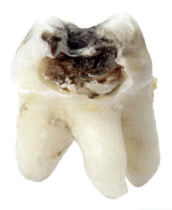

contd

Reducing the risk of dental caries

Maintaining good oral hygiene and, again, following a healthy balanced diet should reduce the risk of dental caries.

Choose unrefined carbohydrate foods such as wholemeal or brown bread, pasta, rice and potatoes, as bacteria find it harder to break these down into acid.

Avoid highly acidic foods, as the acid erodes the enamel. Chewing on sugar-free gum also helps, as it increases saliva production, which in turn helps to disperse the acids in the mouth.

Tips for looking after teeth:

- Brush teeth twice a day with fluoride toothpaste.
- Spend at least 3 minutes each time.
- Ensure you reach right in to the back teeth.
- Visit the dentist regularly.
- Use dental floss.
- Cut down on sugary and starchy snacks.
- Avoid sugary and fizzy drinks.

OBESITY

Obesity is the condition of being very overweight with a very high degree of body fat. This can be caused by having a diet high in fats and sugars and low in fibre (NSP), also by consuming more energy than is used up by activities.

Being overweight can lead to a number of medical problems and conditions:

- high blood pressure
- strokes
- coronary heart disease
- Type 2 diabetes
- some types of cancer
- depression
- joint problems.

Reducing the risk of obesity

The main way to reduce weight-gain and to reduce obesity is to cut down on the amount of energy taken into the body while increasing the amount of energy expended by the body.

The best way to do this is to swap unhealthy and high-energy food choices for healthier choices:

- Check food labels to compare energy content.
- Swap white, refined foods for wholemeal varieties, e.g. bread, rice.
- Swap processed foods and ready meals for fresh varieties.
- Cut down on sugary and salty snacks – e.g. crisps, biscuits, cakes.

DON'T FORGET

Obesity is defined as being 20% (or more) over an individual's ideal bodyweight. **Body Mass Index** (BMI) is commonly used to classify weight in relation to height.

ONLINE TEST

Take the 'Effects of diet-related conditions or diseases on health: Hypertension and strokes, Dental Caries and Obesity' test online at www.brightredbooks.net/N5HFT

THINGS TO DO AND THINK ABOUT

If you want to find out more about your BMI, use the 'Healthy Weight Calculator' at www.brightredbooks.net/N5HFT

EFFECTS OF DIET-RELATED CONDITIONS OR DISEASES ON HEALTH 4

TYPE 2 DIABETES

Diabetes occurs when the body cannot make proper use of the glucose in the blood to convert it into energy. As a result, the amount of glucose (sugar) in the blood starts to rise. Blood glucose levels rise after you have eaten a meal; and a substance called insulin is released. Insulin is a hormone produced by the pancreas. When someone has diabetes, their pancreas does not make enough insulin.

Some people are insulin-dependent (also known as Type 1). This means they need to have daily injections of insulin in order to control their diabetes. About 25% of diabetics are insulin-dependent. Others are non-insulin-dependent (known as Type 2). This type of diabetes is most common in people aged 40+.

Symptoms

The first signs of diabetes are increased thirst and a dry mouth, frequent trips to the toilet, weight loss, tiredness and perhaps blurred vision.

Reducing the risk of diabetes

Many people wrongly believe that eating a diet high in sugar causes diabetes. This is *not* the case; however, it is true that being overweight or obese can increase the risk of suffering from diabetes, so it is important to maintain a healthy weight as well as a healthy diet. This healthy diet should include plenty of total complex carbohydrates, fruit, vegetables and essential fatty acids. Small, regular meals are recommended. Plenty of water should be included in the diet to keep the kidneys working well.

OSTEOPOROSIS

Osteoporosis is also known as 'porous or brittle bones'.

The majority of the calcium in your diet is stored in the bones and teeth. Although bones stop growing by your late teens, they still increase in density until about the age of 30–35. This is when you have reached 'peak bone mass'. After this stage, your bones start to wear down, and you lose more bone than can be replaced.

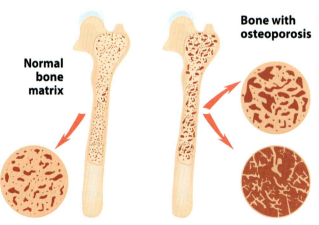

Osteoporosis

Normal bone matrix

Bone with osteoporosis

contd

Women are more likely to suffer from osteoporosis, especially after reaching menopause.

Symptoms

People who suffer from osteoporosis have bones that become very fragile and are more at risk of fracturing. Areas most commonly affected are the hips, spine and wrists. Osteoporosis is often referred to as the silent disease, as you don't know what state your bones are in unless you have a bone-density scan.

Osteoporosis sufferers can lose up to 12cm in height and may start to see a curve in their spine, known as a 'dowager's hump'.

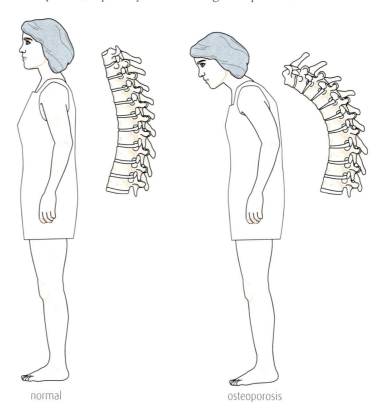

normal   osteoporosis

Prevention/reducing the risk

As calcium is the main component of bone, it is vital to eat a diet high in calcium.

Diet must also include sources of vitamin D, as it controls the absorption of calcium in the body.

Maintaining a healthy weight is important. Thin people, and those suffering from eating disorders, are more prone to osteoporosis.

Regular weight-bearing exercise helps to build and maintain bone, e.g. walking or cycling.

Avoid eating too much salt and drinking caffeine, as these can cause calcium to be excreted in the urine. Also avoid excess alcohol, as alcohol can reduce the absorption of calcium.

VIDEO LINK

Click on the NHS video to find out more about osteoporosis: www.brightredbooks.net/N5HFT

ONLINE TEST

Take the 'Effects of diet-related conditions or diseases on health: Type 2 Diabetes and Osteoporosis' test online at www.brightredbooks.net/N5HFT

THINGS TO DO AND THINK ABOUT

Choose one of the diet-related diseases that you have learned about in this chapter. Undertake some additional research, including finding out: the cost to the NHS of the diet-related disease; whether it is more prevalent among a particular group of people; key causes; symptoms; and suggestions for prevention. Is there any current research being undertaken into the disease/condition? Summarise your findings and present to your classmates in a format of your choice.

Extension Task (1)

Investigate the term *disease of affluence*. What does it mean? Again, summarise your findings and feedback to your class.

Extension Task (2)

Investigate additional diet-related conditions such as kidney or gall stones. Design a poster or leaflet to display your findings.

DIETARY AND HEALTH NEEDS OF DIFFERENT GROUPS

We have seen so far that people need to have a balanced diet that includes a variety of nutrients in order to stay healthy and to reduce the risk of diet-related diseases.

DIETARY REFERENCE VALUES

The amount of each nutrient the body requires is called the 'Nutritional Requirement'. These are different for each nutrient and also vary across different groups of individuals in society.

These requirements are measured by Dietary Reference Values (DRVs).

No two people are the same; however, DRVs give an estimate of the requirements for different groups of healthy people in the UK.

There are three types of estimate:

Estimated Average Requirement (EAR)

This is the estimate of the average need for a nutrient – some people may need to take in more, some people may need less.

Reference Nutrient Intake (RNI)

This is the amount of a nutrient which is sufficient for most of the population.

Lower Reference Nutrient Intake (LRNI)

This is the intake for those who have lower needs than most.

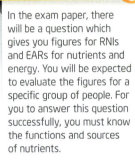

DON'T FORGET

In the exam paper, there will be a question which gives you figures for RNIs and EARs for nutrients and energy. You will be expected to evaluate the figures for a specific group of people. For you to answer this question successfully, you must know the functions and sources of nutrients.

SPECIAL DIETARY NEEDS OF DIFFERENT GROUPS: INFANTS

Any child under the age of 1 is normally classed as an infant.

At this stage of life, growth is rapid, and so a nutritious diet is essential to ensure that the infant stays healthy.

For the first few months of life, an infant should be given only milk. This could be in the form of either breast milk from the mother or formula milk from a bottle.

contd

One of the Scottish Dietary Targets is to encourage more women to breastfeed, as it is considered to be the best start in life for a new baby because:

- breast milk provides the correct composition and proportion for each baby

- the nutrients in breast milk are in a form which is easier for a baby to digest, and it is totally sterile so is less likely to cause infections

- breast milk contains antibodies from the mother which help to protect the baby's immune system

- breast milk is free

- breast milk requires no additional preparation and is provided at the correct consistency and temperature

- breast milk may be expressed and frozen or stored in a refrigerator to allow the mother to have a break

- breastfeeding helps to promote a bond between mother and baby

- breastfeeding also helps the mother to lose any extra weight gained during pregnancy, as it uses extra energy

- it is also thought that breastfeeding helps to reduce the risk to the mother of breast or ovarian cancer in later life.

ONLINE

For more, check out the 'Age-by-age guide to feeding your baby' at www.brightredbooks.net/N5HFT

For some mothers, breastfeeding is not an option, and they choose to use a specially prepared infant formula.

In this case, it is important to ensure that:

- measuring of powder is accurate to ensure that the baby is not overfed or underfed

- all equipment used to prepare and feed the baby is sterilised to prevent infections/food poisoning, which can kill a baby of this age.

Weaning

Infants can be weaned gradually onto solid foods from about 4–6 months old.

When weaning babies it is important to remember that:

- foods should not contain any added salt, sugar or artificial additives

- a source of iron should be included as babies will need this for red blood cell development

- foods should be pureed to prevent choking

- new foods should be introduced gradually to ensure any allergies are picked up quickly

- different textures and flavours should be introduced to ensure the baby has a balanced diet and also to reduce the risk of them becoming a fussy eater.

ONLINE TEST

Take the 'Dietary and Health Needs of Different Groups' test online at www.brightredbooks.net/N5HFT

THINGS TO DO AND THINK ABOUT

1 Look at the information on solid foods for babies at www.brightredbooks.net/N5HFT. Make an information leaflet to inform mothers about the best foods to use to feed their infants.

2 Look at the information in the table about the EAR for energy for infants from the BrightRED Digital Zone. How do the figures compare between boys and girls? Come up with some reasons for any differences.

SPECIFIC DIETARY NEEDS OF DIFFERENT GROUPS 1

CHILDREN

We use the word 'children' to describe boys and girls between the ages of 1 and 10. This is a time of rapid growth in a child's life, and so the requirements for all the major nutrients are high.

During this time, eating habits are formed, and so children should be encouraged to have a healthy, varied diet with low amounts of refined sugar and salt. Fat intake, especially that of saturated fat, should be monitored carefully.

The most important nutrients needed at this stage are:

Nutrient	Dietary need
Protein	This is a time of rapid growth and development, therefore protein is needed for growth and maintenance of all cells. Children often injure themselves, and their bodies need protein to repair cuts and wounds.
Carbohydrate	Total complex carbohydrates should be the main source of energy for children. Children are usually very energetic – boys more so than girls.
Calcium	At this stage, bones and teeth are developing and growing rapidly, and the need for calcium increases with age.
Iron	The volume of blood in the body increases with age and size, therefore a good supply of iron is needed to prevent anaemia. Children who are more active will need a greater intake of iron to ensure that they do not tire easily.
Vitamin C	As children are active, they need a good source of vitamin C to help heal wounds and to help absorb iron to prevent tiredness and anaemia.

DON'T FORGET

Young children often need encouragement to eat healthily, so meals should be small with a variety of flavours, colours and textures.

ONLINE

For more, read the link 'Life stages' at www.brightredbooks.net/N5HFT

DON'T FORGET

Across the majority of nutrient groups, boys have a greater nutrient requirement than girls.

ADOLESCENTS

An adolescent is generally a person between the ages of 11 and 18. This is another period of rapid growth, sometimes called the 'growth spurt', in life – so, again, the intake of the main nutrients needs to increase.

Nutrient	Dietary need
Protein	As this is a period of rapid growth, protein is needed for the growth, repair and maintenance of cells. Many teenagers are very active, therefore will need protein for repair of injuries.
Carbohydrate	Energy needs vary depending upon how active the adolescent is. Energy needs increase as the body frame grows – boys generally need more energy than girls.
Calcium	During adolescence, bone development is at its peak.
Iron	As the body frame grows, so does the volume of blood, therefore iron is required to prevent anaemia. The onset of menstruation for teenage girls means that they will need to increase iron intake to make up for the loss of blood.
Vitamin C	This is important to ensure optimum iron absorption to prevent anaemia.

Many adolescents do not eat a balanced diet. They tend to rely on high-fat, high-salt snacks and fast foods which are energy-dense but low in nutritive value.

ADULTS

At this point in life, body growth has stopped. Many people tend to become less active, and so energy and other nutrient requirements become less; however, due to certain special needs and beliefs, nutrient requirements vary across the adult population.

The majority of healthy adults will require the following:

Nutrient	Dietary need
Protein	Body cells are continually repairing and replacing.
Carbohydrate	As activity generally decreases with age, less energy is required; however, total complex carbohydrate is better than fat. Men require more energy than women, as they tend to be more active than women and have larger body frames.
Calcium	At this stage, bone maintenance is important to help prevent onset of osteoporosis in later life.
Iron	Women in particular still need a good intake of iron to compensate for blood loss through menstruation until onset of menopause.

DON'T FORGET

The dietary targets recommend that adults should reduce the amounts of fat, sugar and saturated fat they eat.

ONLINE TEST

Take the 'Special Dietary Needs for Different Groups: Children, Adolescents and Adults' test online at www.brightredbooks.net/N5HFT

THINGS TO DO AND THINK ABOUT

1   Getting involved in food preparation may help to encourage children to eat more healthily.

    Look at the information on this web page, and watch the video 'Cooking with Kids': www.brightredbooks.net/N5HFT

    Devise a leaflet for parents, including a recipe for your own pizza, to encourage them to safely allow children to help cook in the home. Or you could consider filming your own 'Cooking with Kids' video.

2   Create a healthy dish suitable for adolescents to have as a snack.

3   Look at the dietary reference values for adolescents to find out which nutrients are same for both sexes.

SPECIFIC DIETARY NEEDS OF DIFFERENT GROUPS 2

THE ELDERLY

As people age, they generally become less active and therefore need less energy. Nevertheless, they still need well-balanced diets to ensure that they are healthy and that they take in all the nutrients they need to maintain and repair their bodies.

Nutrient	Dietary need
Protein	As elderly people often suffer from ill health, protein is needed to help repair cells and aid recovery.
Carbohydrate	Energy needs reduce, but total complex carbohydrate and NSP are still important to help reduce the risk of constipation and obesity.
Calcium	As the body ages, bone density reduces, and a good supply of calcium – along with vitamin D and phosphorus – is important to reduce the risk of osteoporosis and osteomalacia.
Iron	The elderly are susceptible to anaemia and, as a result, need to take in a good source of iron.

When planning meals for the elderly, it is useful to consider the following:

- Elderly people often have digestive problems, therefore it is important that foods are not too highly spiced or fatty, as this may increase the problem.

- Many elderly people have dentures, therefore it is useful to avoid foods which are hard to chew. Any fruit and vegetables which are very firm should be lightly cooked/ steamed to soften them.

- Lower-fat alternatives to dairy produce should be used to cut down on energy content but keep up the calcium content to help maintenance of teeth and bones.

Foods to be avoided

- Salt should be avoided to help prevent high blood pressure – stroke is a real risk to the elderly.

- Unpasteurised dairy produce, e.g. milk or certain cheeses, should be avoided to reduce the risk of food poisoning.

DON'T FORGET

Many elderly people suffer from diet-related problems due to their age and lifestyle. Some of these can be helped by following a balanced diet and reducing the salt, saturated fat and sugar content of the diet.

PREGNANT WOMEN

Pregnant women have special dietary needs, as they have to meet not only their own nutritional needs but also the needs of their growing baby.

Nutrient	Dietary need
Protein	Needed for the growth of the baby's cells.
Carbohydrate	Important in the last three months of pregnancy due to the rapid growth and development of the baby. However, care should be taken not to eat too much to prevent excessive weight-gain which may be difficult to lose after the birth.
Iron	There is no need for increased intake of iron in pregnancy, as menstruation stops; however, as the mother's blood supply is used to supply the baby with iron for the first few weeks of life, it is essential that a good intake of iron is maintained.
Vitamin C	Vitamin C is need to help tissue formation in the baby. It is also useful to help with absorption of iron.
Folic acid	Folic acid is essential in the first three months of pregnancy to prevent neural tube defects (spina bifida) in the developing foetus. It also helps to prevent anaemia.
Calcium	Along with phosphorus and vitamin D, calcium is essential for maintaining the skeleton of the mother but is also used to ensure the development of the skeleton in the baby. If the mother does not have a good intake of calcium, the developing baby will take what it needs from the mother's bones, potentially causing weakness.
NSP	Although NSP (fibre) is not a nutrient, the mother needs to maintain a good intake, as women are more susceptible to constipation and haemorrhoids during pregnancy.

contd

When planning meals, pregnant women should avoid certain foods:

- Foods with a high vitamin A content, such as liver or liver products like pâté – too much vitamin A is harmful to both the mother and the developing baby.
- Soft cheeses like Brie and Camembert – they may contain a bacteria called Listeria.
- Raw eggs, and foods containing raw eggs, such as home-made mayonnaise, should be avoided due to the risk of salmonella bacteria.

VEGETARIANS

Many people in society choose to be vegetarian. There are many different types of vegetarians today who eat a variety of different foods; however, the most common types of vegetarian are:

- lacto-vegetarian: do not eat fish, meat, meat products or eggs, but will consume milk and other dairy produce.
- vegan: do not eat/use any product which has come from an animal.

Special dietary needs – lacto-vegetarian

As lacto-vegetarians eat milk and cheese, they still maintain a reasonable intake of protein and calcium. Lower-fat options of dairy produce should be chosen, as the increased intake of these foods in place of meat and fish could lead to a higher intake of saturated fat. Lacto-vegetarians may find they have a reduced intake of iron, as they do not eat red meat, which is a major source. Care should be taken to ensure that enough iron is taken in to reduce the risk of anaemia.

Special dietary needs – vegan

As with all well-planned diets, good vegan diets are rich in whole plant foods, vital for fibre. Vegans can easily exceed Government 'Five a Day' guidelines for brightly coloured vegetables and fruits. Choose a range of protein foods such as legumes, grains and nuts over each week to easily meet WHO (World Health Organisation) healthy protein intake. Include calcium foods such as green leafy vegetables and calcium-fortified plant milks.

Everyone over the age of 50 - on any diet - needs vitamin B12 first-hand from the micro-organisms which make it, from reliable fortified foods or supplements. Vegans of all ages get vitamin B12 in this way.

Many people in the UK don't get enough vitamin D from their diets. North of Birmingham, it is hard to get enough vitamin D from healthy sun exposure. So, anyone who lives in Scotland - including vegans - needs sufficient vitamin D from reliable fortified foods and supplements. (Most vitamin D comes from sheep's lanolin, so is not suitable for vegans; vitamin D from plants is suitable for vegans always check the label for the source used or look for the vegan symbol).

THINGS TO DO AND THINK ABOUT

1 If the elderly contract food poisoning, the results could be fatal. Devise a list of hygiene rules to follow when preparing food for the elderly to ensure their safety.

2 Find out why Listeria bacteria is so harmful to pregnant women and their developing babies.

3 Use the internet to research the Healthy Start scheme. Find out which nutrients are available on this scheme, and give their functions in the diet of a pregnant woman.

Plan and prepare a healthy meal for a pregnant woman. Show how it is suitable by creating a chart of its nutritional content, and compare it to the DRV for pregnant women.

4 Find out why some people choose to adopt a vegetarian diet. Show your findings in a PowerPoint presentation or leaflet.

DON'T FORGET

Lactose is the main carbohydrate in milk. Lacto-vegetarians won't eat meat or meat products but *will* eat milk and dairy produce. Some people are lactose-intolerant, i.e. they have an adverse reaction to cow's milk.

ONLINE

Check out the 'Vegetarian Eatwell Plate' at www.brightredbooks.net/N5HFT

ONLINE TEST

Take the 'Special Dietary Needs for Different Groups: Elderly, Pregnant Women, Vegans and Vegetarians' test online at www.brightredbooks.net/N5HFT

PERSONAL HYGIENE AND SAFETY

You must be able to explain appropriate standards of personal hygiene and safety necessary when carrying out food-production tasks.

PERSONAL HYGIENE

Personal hygiene relates to the person handling the food. An important way to prevent food contamination is to maintain a high standard of personal hygiene and cleanliness.

Even healthy people carry food-poisoning bacteria on their bodies. By touching parts of your body, such as your nose, mouth or hair (where you find a bacterium called *Staphylococcus aureus*), or your clothes, you can spread bacteria from your hands to the food.

Prevent the spread of bacteria that can lead to food poisoning by practising good personal hygiene:

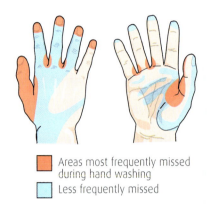

■ Areas most frequently missed during hand washing
■ Less frequently missed
□ Not missed

Bacteria on hands

- Thoroughly wash and dry your hands with soap and hot water before handling food, after using the toilet and if you need to blow your nose. Don't forget to wash and dry them again frequently during food production.

- Dry your hands with clean towels, disposable paper towels or under an air dryer.

- Never smoke, chew gum, spit or eat/drink in a food-handling or food-storage area.

- Never cough or sneeze over food or where food is prepared or stored.

- Fingers should not be licked. Care should be taken not to touch your nose/mouth/hair; if you do, you must wash your hands straight away.

- Wear clean protective clothing, such as an apron.

- Clean protective clothing should only be worn in the food-preparation area and should be washed daily.

- Keep your spare clothes and other personal items away from where food is stored and prepared.

- If you have long hair, tie it back or cover it.

- Keep your nails short so they are easy to clean, and don't wear nail polish or false nails, as varnish can chip into the food, or false nails could come loose.

- Avoid wearing jewellery, or only wear plain banded rings and sleeper earrings.

- If you have cuts or wounds, make sure they are completely covered by a waterproof wound strip or a bandage. Use brightly coloured (blue) wound strips, so they can be seen easily if they fall off.

- Wear disposable gloves over the top of the wound strip if you have wounds on your hands.

- Change disposable gloves regularly.

- Advise your supervisor if you feel unwell – and don't handle food. If you have a problem that relates to your nose, skin, throat or stomach, or bowel trouble or an infected wound, it is a legal requirement that you inform your supervisor.

ONLINE

Revision notes on this topic are available at www.brightredbooks.net/N5HFT

VIDEO LINK

Why not watch the video at www.brightredbooks.net/N5HFT to find out more about the importance of hand-washing in food hygiene?

DON'T FORGET

Knowledge shown should relate to *personal hygiene* and not kitchen hygiene, so think about the rules *you* should follow when you are preparing food to make sure it is safe to eat.

FOOD SAFETY

Food hygiene and safety is extremely important when producing any food product. Food must be safe to eat – and, to do so, potential hazards must be avoided. In a food product, a hazard is anything that is likely to cause harm. These include biological, chemical and physical hazards.

Food spoilage is the process in which food deteriorates to the point that it is unfit for consumption. Food that spoils is referred to as perishable. Food spoilage is caused by the action of enzymes and micro-organisms.

Enzymes

Enzymes are made from amino acids (the building blocks of protein). Enzymes can cause food to ripen, to brown and to oxidise, causing the loss of certain nutrients.

Micro-organisms

Three main micro-organisms are bacteria, moulds and yeast. Bacteria are single-celled organisms that are not visible to the naked eye. Some bacteria can be harmful and can cause food to spoil. Harmful bacteria that cause food poisoning are known as 'pathogens'.

All micro-organisms require certain conditions to grow. These conditions are:

- Food – bacteria prefer high-protein, perishable foods such as meat or dairy produce.
- Moisture – without moisture, bacteria cannot grow, hence the reason dried foods have a longer shelf life.
- Oxygen – some bacteria need oxygen to grow and multiply (known as 'aerobic'), while some grow best without oxygen (known as 'anaerobic').
- pH – most bacteria prefer a neutral pH, and cannot grow in strongly alkaline or acidic conditions. For example, pickling eggs in vinegar extends their shelf life.
- Time – bacteria can multiply rapidly, given time and the right conditions. One bacterium can split into two every 20 minutes via a process called binary fission.
- Temperature – bacteria need warmth in order to grow and multiply. The 'danger zone' for rapid bacterial growth is between 5° and 63°C. Bacteria are dormant at very cold temperatures (such as –18°C in the freezer), grow very slowly at fridge temperature of 0–5°C and are destroyed at temperatures above 63°C.

The Food Safety Act 1990 covers the whole food chain from farm to fork. It makes sure that all food produced and sold is safe to eat.

Food must not be: – injurious to health
                 – unfit for consumption
                 – contaminated.

The day-to-day enforcement of the Food Safety Act is carried out by Environmental Health Officers, who focus on the hygiene of food premises and food safety, and by Trading Standards Officers, who focus on weights and measures, food labelling and the composition of food. The role of Environmental Health and Trading Standards is covered in Unit 3, pages 78-79.

ONLINE

If you want to explore the role of enzymes in the body further, look at the following web links: 'How cells work' and 'Enzymes and digestion' at www.brightredbooks.net/N5HFT

THINGS TO DO AND THINK ABOUT

1   Design a display for the classroom that highlights all the conditions bacteria need to grow.

2   Imagine you are employed by your local council as an Environmental Health Officer. You have been asked to visit a local takeaway, as a customer has complained that they felt unwell after eating food they bought there. You find the following: the fridge is packed full of uncovered raw chicken alongside salad vegetables. The fridge temperature is 12°C. Your task is to write a report on your findings, highlighting areas of concern and actions the takeaway must take to improve their food-safety standards.

ONLINE TEST

Take the 'Personal hygiene and safety' test online at www.brightredbooks.net/N5HFT

FUNCTIONAL PROPERTIES OF FOOD 1

Ingredients have a range of different *properties* – also called *functions*.

The main nutrient provided by an ingredient gives it a range of properties during cooking. Functional properties of different foods can be combined to give various different effects.

To succeed at National 5, you will be required to know about properties of the following nutrients:

- Carbohydrate
- Protein
- Fat.

CARBOHYDRATE

Carbohydrate foods are always of plant origin.

Starch is present in foods such as: potatoes, flour, bread, rice and pasta.

Sugars are naturally present in foods such as: milk, fruits, vegetables, honey.

FUNCTIONAL PROPERTIES OF STARCH

(1) Gelatinisation/Thickening

Starch does not dissolve in water until heat is applied. At about 60°C, the starch grains begin to absorb water. At about 85°C, the grains have absorbed about five times their volume in water. Eventually, so much water is absorbed that the starch grains swell and burst, and a **gel** is formed.

Gelatinisation is used in thickening sauces, soups, custard and so on. Also, when starch gelatinises it helps to produce moist baked products with a good texture and volume. Here the starch grains absorb mixture from the bread or cake dough; and, as the temperature rises, these gelatinise and set.

(2) Dextrinisation/Browning

Starch helps baked products like bread and cakes to become brown. When starch is subjected to dry heat, a chemical change takes place. The starch molecules break down into dextrin.

(3) Fermentation

Bread is usually made from 'strong' flour, i.e. flour with a high gluten (protein) content. The elasticity (ability to stretch) of the gluten enables the yeast dough to stretch and to hold the carbon dioxide gas, produced during fermentation, in small pockets which in turn allows the bread to rise.

Glucose → Carbon dioxide + Alcohol + Energy

Bread becomes toast through dextrinisation.

DON'T FORGET

Dextrins are starch chains made up of glucose molecules.

DON'T FORGET

Fermentation is the process by which yeast is able to obtain energy through the breakdown of glucose without requiring oxygen.

VIDEO LINK

Watch the bread-making process from start to finish here: www.brightredbooks.net/N5HFT

FUNCTIONAL PROPERTIES OF SUGAR

(1) Aeration

This is the process of trapping air. When sugar is added to fat and creamed, the crystals of sugar cut into the fat, and air is added via beating. The fat surrounds the air bubbles and traps them. Using caster sugar means more air bubbles are produced as the sugar crystals are finer, but icing sugar does not work so well (nor do some artificial sweeteners) as the crystals are just too small.

(2) Caramelisation

When sugar is heated, it melts and a caramel is formed. Overheating the mixture will result in it burning. Caramel can be formed by melting sugar alone – or, by first dissolving sugar in water, then applying heat, the water is driven off and a caramel is formed. It is usually used in confectionery.

(3) Crystallisation

When sugar and water are boiled, the water is driven off and a thick syrup is formed. This sets on cooling, i.e. reverts to its crystal form. When used in products such as tablet or fudge, the mixture is beaten as it cools so that smaller crystals form, which provides a smoother texture.

(4) Dextrinisation/Browning

Sugar and amino acids in protein interact in baked products, e.g. when baking a cake or roasting meat. This is known as non-enzymic browning or the Maillard reaction, after the French scientist who discovered it.

Caramelised sugar

(5) Flavouring/Sweetening

The sweet flavour of sugar is used to sweeten a variety of products, including some processed foods like beans and tomato sauce. It can also reduce the sharp acidic taste of some foods, e.g. adding to rhubarb when stewing.

(6) Preservation

High concentrations of sugar can be used to prevent the growth of micro-organisms and are therefore used as a preservative in foods such as jam, marmalade and some canned fruit. This is due to the fact that sugar has a dehydrating effect, and micro-organisms cannot grow in the absence of moisture.

ONLINE

For more on the properties and functions of sugar, watch the e-seminar: www.brightredbooks.net/N5HFT

ONLINE TEST

How well do you know the properties of carbohydrate foods? Test yourself online at www.brightredbooks.net/N5HFT

THINGS TO DO AND THINK ABOUT

Investigate the effect of sugar on a cake recipe. Use a standard 50g self-raising flour/fat/sugar to 1 egg recipe as a control. Change the amounts and types of sugar – try using artificial sugar in one mixture. Compare the results. Write a brief report on your findings.

Experiment with different types of starches by making a basic white sauce (25g fat, 25g starch, 250ml milk) using, for example, wheat flour, rice flour, tapioca, cornflour and arrowroot. Compare the results. Reflect on the differences in taste, appearance and texture.

FUNCTIONAL PROPERTIES OF FOOD 2

DON'T FORGET

Chains of amino acids = building blocks of protein.

PROTEIN

Most foods contain some protein. For example, collagen is the protein in meat, gluten is the protein in wheat, albumen is the protein in egg-white. Some types of protein help with the reactions that happen when food is cooked. These are known as enzymes.

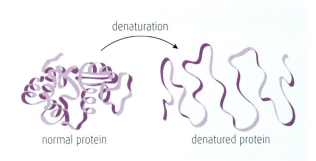

normal protein   denatured protein

FUNCTIONAL PROPERTIES OF PROTEIN

(1) Aeration

Aeration is evident when making meringue. Meringue is made from whipped egg-white and sugar. As the eggs are whisked, air bubbles are beaten into the liquid, and the protein in egg **denatures**. These denatured protein strands make the mixture more stable. Egg-white alone can trap as much as 7 times its own volume in air. This is called a **foam**. Adding sugar increases the time it takes to produce a foam because it slows down the denaturation of the egg-white protein. It's always best to beat the egg-white on its own to a soft peak before starting to add the sugar.

Creaming

Aeration process	Description
Whisking/whipping/beating	Agitating protein will cause it to denature. The protein structure unwinds, and air is trapped. This creates a foam, such as when egg-white is whisked to make meringue.
Sieving	When flour is sieved, the particles incorporate air.
Rubbing in	When you rub fat into flour, the fat coats the flour particles and reduces the amount of water that can be absorbed. Air is trapped when doing so. Lifting the mixture up while rubbing in also serves to add extra air to the mixture.
Creaming	When fat and sugar are creamed together, the sugar crystals are cut into the fat, causing the fat molecules to split, enabling air to be incorporated. The lighter and fluffier the mixture, the more air is trapped.
Addition of liquids	When heated, liquids change to steam. This steam will expand and rise, allowing the food product to increase in volume.
Rolling and folding	When making puff or flaky pastry, air is trapped by the action of rolling and folding the pastry dough.

Rolling and folding

(2) Binding

A binding agent is an ingredient that holds all the other ingredients together in a product, for example egg. Egg proteins coagulate when heated and bind ingredients together, for example in burgers or fishcakes.

(3) Coagulation

On the application of heat, at around 60°C, proteins begin to change. This process is called denaturation, i.e. the proteins change in appearance (think about when you cook egg-white and it changes from opaque to white). When the protein in meat denatures, the muscle fibres become firmer; and, beyond 60°C, the fibres shrink and the meat juices are driven off. Overcooking means that the meat will become tough.

When water is added to flour, gluten is produced. Gluten stretches easily and becomes more elastic the more it is worked (kneaded). When bread dough is heated, the gluten is stretched by bubbles of gas produced by the yeast, making the bread rise. The gluten then coagulates, i.e. sets. Once protein has coagulated, the changes are irreversible.

contd

(4) Glazing

A shiny brown top to a product like a scone can be achieved if beaten egg is brushed on top before cooking.

(5) Thickening

Gelatine is a protein that is extracted from collagen in meat. Gelatine melts to a liquid when heated but sets to a gel on cooling. It is found in products such as fruit gums and marshmallows.

FAT

Fats are made up of the same elements as carbohydrates – carbon, hydrogen and oxygen – but in different proportions. They are found in both animal and plant foods, such as butter, lard, meat, cream, peanuts, olives or sunflower seeds.

Fats are classified according to the amount of hydrogen they contain, with the two main groups of fat being:

- **saturated fats**, which contain the maximum amount of hydrogen – solid at room temperature
- **unsaturated fats**, which do not contain the maximum amount of hydrogen – liquid at room temperature.

FUNCTIONAL PROPERTIES OF FAT

(1) Aeration

Solid fats (such as soft margarine) will trap bubbles of air when creamed or beaten with sugar. Sugar granules cut into the fat, producing air bubbles, which the fat surrounds and traps.

(2) Emulsification

Emulsification is the property that allows fats and oils to mix with water, preventing them from separating out. Lecithin, found in egg-yolk, is a natural emulsifier. Mayonnaise is an emulsion of oil and vinegar which has been stabilised by egg-yolk.

(3) Preservation

Fat helps to extend the shelf-life of baked products like cakes and bread due to fat's function of allowing the product to retain moisture. Lower-fat products tend to dry out very quickly and will not keep for any length of time.

(4) Shortening

Fats and oils help to 'shorten' a flour mixture such as pastry or shortbread so as to give it a crisp/crumbly melt-in-the-mouth texture. The greater the proportion of fat to flour, the shorter/crumblier the texture will be. It works via the fat coating the flour, reducing the amount of water which is absorbed. Animal fats, such as butter and lard, are the best shortening agents.

 THINGS TO DO AND THINK ABOUT

Design a recipe that has the greatest number of functional properties that you can include. Produce and reflect on your product ☺☺☺.

For more activites on the functional properties of food, turn to page 92.

 VIDEO LINK

Watch the clip about how to apply an egg wash: www.brightredbooks.net/N5HFT

 **DON'T FORGET**

Fats are, strictly speaking, **lipids** that are solid at room temperature.
Oils are **lipids** that are liquid at room temperature.

 **ONLINE TEST**

How well do you know the properties of protein and fat? Test yourself online at www.brightredbooks.net/N5HFT

STAGES OF FOOD PRODUCT DEVELOPMENT

VIDEO LINK

Follow the link from the BrightRED Digital Zone to view an e-seminar on product direction and trends for the Marks & Spencer Food Group.

ONLINE

For more information about food product development, check out 'Product development' at www.brightredbooks.net/N5HFT

VIDEO LINK

Watch the clip about how Sainsbury's develop new food products: www.brightredbooks.net/N5HFT

DON'T FORGET

A **design brief** is a defined situation/statement that outlines guidelines for the task.

DON'T FORGET

Manufacturers use different ways to come up with new ideas. You might want to look at mind-mapping or at recipes or food magazines and create a mood board to help you dream up initial ideas.

ONLINE

Look at the case study on The New Covent Garden Soup Company: www.brightredbooks.net/N5HFT. Undertake some of the tasks listed there aimed at developing understanding of food product development.

OVERVIEW

Each year, around 10 000 new food and drink products are launched in the UK. Around 90% fail. Very few products are totally 'new'. Mostly they are produced by modifying an existing product.

Foods are developed in a number of stages. First, there must be a concept for the product. Manufacturers in the food industry have lots of different ways they can come up with new ideas, such as:

- analysing consumers' trends and eating habits
- researching what restaurants/cafés are serving
- using foreign travel to bring back new foreign food ideas
- modifying existing products for specific target groups – such as adapting to meet healthy-eating targets or specific dietary needs
- experimental work in the test kitchen with unusual/new/novel ingredients
- adapting existing products to give line extension, or copying an existing product to make an 'own brand'
- seeking views from focus groups.

Usually, in food-manufacturing companies, the marketing department will use their research to provide the product-development team with **a design brief** for the type of product they want, e.g. a sandwich that will help customers to stay healthy and live longer.

CONCEPT GENERATION

This is the thinking stage. Development of ideas comes from activities such as market analysis, or perhaps looking at popular existing products to see how they can be adapted or improved. When research is undertaken or information gathered, it is known as investigating. It is important to identify a need. By asking, and considering, what people want, a target market can be identified.

CONCEPT SCREENING

This is a filtering stage. All initial design ideas are considered. Some are rejected as being too complicated, expensive, unhealthy or boring, or because they just won't work. The ideas that are left are considered to be the most suitable to go forward to the next stage of the process.

At this point, the design team may note a description of each idea and give reasons why they think each idea might meet the needs of the brief. This is sometimes called a 'specification' or a product plan.

A description of the design idea (specification) is a list of points explaining what you want your product to be like. It could include the target group the product is aimed at; a description of the product; what the product should look, smell and taste like; the sort of ingredients the product will contain; any sort of storage points or packaging ideas; cost; any special nutritional requirements or allergy implications.

EXAMPLE:

A description/product plan/specification for a healthy sandwich might include:
- Aimed at busy, professional people
- Wholegrain bread, range of seasonal fillings, containing salad vegetables

contd

- Colourful, lots of filling visible, full of flavour with a variety of textures
- Priced around £3.00
- Recyclable cardboard packaging with window to view product
- Low in fat and salt but high in fibre and vegetables to meet current dietary advice.

PROTOTYPE PRODUCTION

A prototype is a sample of what the developed product will look like.

Prototype production often takes place in a test kitchen. At this stage, you may want to consider making more than one prototype of the idea that best meets the design idea. For example, if you were asked to develop a healthy cake that includes a vegetable ingredient, you might want to experiment with your basic recipe and add parsnip to one, courgette to another, beetroot to a third and pumpkin to a fourth cake. By doing so, it gives you more to take to the testing panel for feedback on their appeal.

PRODUCT TESTING

The product prototype(s) are tested on consumers so that their opinions can be gathered. Feedback is used to refine the product further; or it may be rejected if feedback from the testers is very negative.

Sensory analysis is used to test the product(s). Sensory analysis is the process of using the senses to evaluate food samples, in a controlled environment, and to record the results.

FIRST PRODUCTION RUN

At this stage, the product goes into production for the first time. It allows the product to be tested to make sure the food manufacturer is happy with the quality. If any factors are unsatisfactory, changes can be made.

MARKETING PLAN

At this stage, the company needs to work out how it is going to promote the product to the target market. There are four main factors to consider when marketing a product. These are known as the **4Ps**.

- **Product** – what is the product all about? What is its unique selling point? What type of packaging will be used?
- **Price** – what is the best price at which to pitch the product so that it sells but also makes a profit? Should it be sold at a low, introductory price or at a premium price to represent quality to fit in with the target market?
- **Place** – where is the product to be sold? A larger supermarket chain? A small corner shop? Specialist deli? One geographic part of the country? How and where will it be displayed within the shop?
- **Promotion** – it is vital that the product is promoted effectively so that as many customers as possible hear about it and buy it, thus maximising sales. Possible promotion techniques include magazine/newspaper/television advertising; in-store demonstration/free samples; money-off coupons; free recipe card; special offers, such as BOGOF (Buy One, Get One Free).

LAUNCH

The product is now on sale. It may be piloted in a small area to gauge interest before launching country-wide. Market research will be undertaken so as to provide feedback on how the product is being received by customers.

VIDEO LINK

Watch the clip about taking ideas to test kitchens: www.brightredbooks.net/N5HFT

VIDEO LINK

For a great look at how sensory testing works in practice, check out the clip at the BrightRED Digital Zone!

VIDEO LINK

Have a look at the video about a pilot production line: www.brightredbooks.net/N5HFT

DON'T FORGET

USP = Unique Selling Point – a marketing concept that aims to show something about the product that will make it stand out to consumers and will set it apart from the competition.

ONLINE TEST

Check how well you know the stages of food product development online at www.brightredbooks.net/N5HFT

VIDEO LINK

Check out the clip about launching a food product: www.brightredbooks.net/N5HFT

THINGS TO DO AND THINK ABOUT

For some activites on the stages of food product development, turn to page 92.

UNDERTAKING INVESTIGATIONS TO GENERATE IDEAS FOR FOOD PRODUCTS 1

In order to develop or design a new food product, manufacturers need to gather information that allows them to go about finding solutions to meet consumers' needs, or to fill a need that they didn't know they had! As well as the market need, it also provides important information in relation to the market size and competition.

There are two major types of **market research**:

1) **Primary research**, subdivided into **quantitative** and **qualitative** research

2) **Secondary research**.

VIDEO LINK

For a further definition of quantitative research, watch 'Quantitative Research' at www.brightredbooks.net/N5HFT

VIDEO LINK

Check out the BrightRED Digital Zone for an explanation of qualitative research.

VIDEO LINK

Watch the clip to see a definition of a focus group: www.brightredbooks.net/N5HFT

VIDEO LINK

Learn more about secondary data by watching the clip at the BrightRED Digital Zone.

DON'T FORGET

In order to get the best possible results from your research, it is important to do as many different types of research as possible. This will help you when it comes to completing the course assignment.

PRIMARY RESEARCH

Primary research involves the collection of original data through activities such as conducting interviews or getting people to complete a questionnaire. Experimental work, such as product disassembly and tasting/testing sessions, would be part of primary research.

Quantitative

This means surveying large numbers of people by questionnaires and interviews to obtain statistical data.

Qualitative

This means asking small groups of people for their opinions on products.

A **focus group** is usually made up of ten or fewer people who are asked interview questions about their perceptions, opinions and attitudes towards a product or concept. Questions are asked in an interactive way, with group discussion allowed.

SECONDARY RESEARCH

Secondary research uses the primary research of others, typically in the form of research publications and reports. Secondary sources could include previous research reports, newspaper, magazine and journal content, and government statistics.

Websites such as Mintel, http://foodanddrink.mintel.com/, government data such as Family Food survey, http://www.defra.gov.uk/statistics/foodfarm/food/familyfood/, The Food People, http://www.thefoodpeople.co.uk/food-trends and British Nutrition Foundation, http://www.nutrition.org.uk/publications/briefingpapers, are all examples of sources that could be accessed to provide secondary data when undertaking an investigation linked to developing a new food product.

TYPES OF INVESTIGATIONS

Once you have decided on the types of market research you are going to undertake, it is time to consider the method by which you will obtain your data.

Interviews

- The suitability of the person to be interviewed should be carefully considered.

- A minimum of five relevant questions should be asked to allow relevant data to be collected.

- Open questions should be used to allow more data to be collected from the interviewee. Open questions can have any answer. However, it is easier to analyse the response to a closed question, so question choice should be considered carefully.

- Questions should be thought out so as to extract useful facts and avoid one-word responses such as 'yes/no'.

Questionnaires

- In order to gather relevant data, a minimum of 20 respondents should be surveyed.

- A minimum of five questions should be included in the questionnaire. The type of question asked is vitally important in order to gain the most useful data.

- When interpreting the results of the data collected, all question and all possible answers must be displayed, including nil responses.

- Results could be displayed as charts or graphs if desired, although this is not necessary. Using a table format to display results often makes interpreting the results easier.

Survey

- A survey is a way of gathering information. It may focus on factual information, or it could be used to collect opinions.

- The source(s) of information should be identified to make the research valid. Possible sources include the internet, literary resources, shops or restaurants, depending upon the product-development brief.

- More than one source should be used.

- Results could be displayed as bullet points or charts/graphs if desired, although this is not necessary. Using a table format to display results often makes interpreting the results easier.

ONLINE

Why not try conducting your research via using an online survey tool? Find examples at www.brightredbooks.net/N5HFT

ONLINE TEST

Check how well you have learned about market research online at www.brightredbooks.net/N5HFT

THINGS TO DO AND THINK ABOUT

Why not try undertaking the following task to put your investigative skills into practice?

1 Select a dietary disease from the following list: Obesity, Coronary Heart Disease, Anaemia, Osteoporosis and Tooth Decay.

2 Using a literary or internet search, find out as much as you can about your chosen disease. Make sure you find out about any specific links to diet. Record your findings.

3 Develop a survey that contains five questions that ask fellow pupils (or teachers) for their views on your chosen disease. For example, have they ever suffered from it? How much do they know about it? Record your findings.

4 Produce a PowerPoint presentation/poster/leaflet/radio or film clip that will allow you to share your findings with your classmates.

UNDERTAKING INVESTIGATIONS TO GENERATE IDEAS FOR FOOD PRODUCTS 2

TYPES OF QUESTIONS

There are two types of survey questions typically used in a quantitative research; **closed questions** and **open questions**. Closed questions are the ones where you have several response options to choose between, while open questions are where you ask respondents to use their own words to explain their thoughts or feelings. Open questions are commonly used in qualitative research; however, they can also be used in quantitative research to get more information and insight into an issue.

Closed questions

Single-choice questions are when you ask respondents to choose one answer, from a list of alternatives, that best describes how they feel about a certain topic. An example of a single-choice question would be: *Which of the following best describes how appealing or unappealing you find product X? Please tick ✔ one.*

Very appealing	☐
Fairly appealing	☐
Neither appealing nor unappealing	☐
Fairly unappealing	☐
Very unappealing	☐

Multi-choice questions are when you ask respondents to pick a number of responses from a pre-constructed list. The following is an example of a multi-choice question:

*Which of the following features do you think product X should include? Tick ✔ **all** that apply.*

Feature A ☐   Feature B ☐   Feature C ☐   Feature D ☐

Closed questions allow for quick responses that are easily analysed, and they are far easier for respondents to answer. However, there are several disadvantages to closed questions. A closed question assumes that you know all the answers and you are just asking respondents to pick one. There is no opportunity to gain insight into why the respondent has answered in the way they have. One way around this might be to give respondents the option of 'Other – please state ...'.

Open questions

An open question gives the respondent an opportunity to provide a range of answers that the researcher may not have considered. Obviously these are key to qualitative interviewing, but they can also be used in quantitative research to give more depth and insight. Consider asking questions that begin with 'Why? How? What do you think about? Tell me about ...'.

For example, you could ask: *Why do you think product X is appealing? Or what is it about product Y that you find appealing/do not find appealing?*

Open questions can be very time-consuming and complicated to analyse. You need to read all or most of them to get an idea of themes that may be coming through. If you want to quantify them, you will need to read them all and put them into sub-headings, and then count the number of times each idea is mentioned, and maybe use one or two direct quotes which sum up the main ideas in your evaluation of the results.

DISASSEMBLY

Disassembly is the process of taking something apart and looking at the individual parts.

contd

DON'T FORGET

Keep questions simple. Do not include any overlapping responses. Never ask a leading question.

What are the purposes of product disassembly?

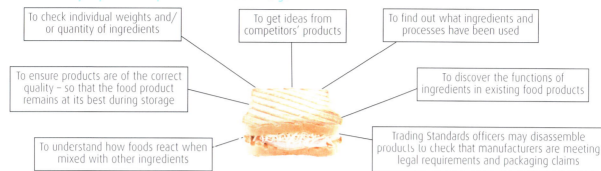

To check individual weights and/or quantity of ingredients

To get ideas from competitors' products

To find out what ingredients and processes have been used

To ensure products are of the correct quality – so that the food product remains at its best during storage

To discover the functions of ingredients in existing food products

To understand how foods react when mixed with other ingredients

Trading Standards officers may disassemble products to check that manufacturers are meeting legal requirements and packaging claims

INTERNET/LITERARY SEARCH

- All sources must be clearly identified – state the URL.

- Data collected should be valid and relevant, ideally sourced from more than one source.

- Information should not be lifted 'en bloc' from websites; it is appropriate to summarise key points which are relevant to the aim of the investigation.

EXAMPLE:

Develop a <u>sandwich</u> *suitable for someone suffering from a* <u>food allergy</u>.

Investigation: To carry out a literary/internet search to find out the most common food allergens.

Information gathered:

http://www.nutrition.org.uk/attachments/209_Food%20allergy%20and%20intolerance%20summary.pdf

From this British Nutrition Foundation briefing paper, I found out that only 1–2% of the population suffer from food allergies/intolerances. The main foods that cause problems are gluten in wheat, lactose in cow's milk, and peanuts.

The Food Book by Jenny Ridgwell (ISBN 978-0-435467-95-1)

Page 19: 'Peanuts, milk and eggs are common food allergens.'

Food and Nutrition by Anita Tull (ISBN 0-19-832766-8)

Page 72: 'In food, the allergen is often a protein. Allergies to cow's milk, eggs, soya and monosodium glutamate are fairly common. Some allergic reactions can be very serious.'

ONLINE TEST

Check how well you know about undertaking investigations online at www.brightredbooks.net/N5HFT

THINGS TO DO AND THINK ABOUT

Case Study

Fraser Doherty from Edinburgh started making jam at home. He realised the importance of researching the existing market – and, by doing so, he found out that sales of jam had been in decline and that the market perceived jam as unhealthy, high in sugar and a product for old people. This vital market research allowed him to see a gap in the market, which he used to develop his low-sugar 'Super Jam'.

VIDEO LINK

Watch the video clip about Super Jam: www.brightredbooks.net/N5HFT

Undertake your own primary research. You can do this by undertaking an interview/focus-group session or developing a questionnaire to seek consumers' views on jam. Incorporate the results of your research into completing the following product-development task – *Develop a low-sugar fruit jam.*

SENSORY TESTING: CONDUCTING SENSORY EVALUATION

Sensory evaluation involves using one or more tests to assess people's responses to different characteristics of food.

Tasting a product is essential if a manufacturer wants to judge how successful a product might be. Often, a trained tasting panel is used to provide feedback on how a product looks, smells, tastes and feels in the mouth.

DON'T FORGET

Hedonic descriptions describe likes and dislikes, e.g. tasty, unpleasant.
Sensory descriptions describe texture, taste, smell or appearance, e.g. greasy, fruity, shiny.
Attitudinal descriptions describe beliefs about a product, e.g. healthy, traditional.

DON'T FORGET

When you are setting up a tasting session in school, you will need to be prepared in advance.
A tasting kit might include the following:
- plain white plates/bowls
- pens/paper
- teaspoons/cutlery
- labels
- cups/bottled water
- paper towels.

WHY USE SENSORY EVALUATION?

It can be used to:
- find out what customers think of new products being developed
- evaluate a range of existing dishes/food products – possibly the competition's dishes
- compare similarities or differences in a range of dishes/food products
- gain feedback on specific characteristics in order to undertake improvements
- check to see if the dish/food product meets its original plan or specification
- check if the product is still acceptable if cheaper ingredients are used or if the fat/sugar/salt content is lowered.

HOW TO SET UP A SENSORY TEST SESSION

- Train testers – the people tasting the food need to know what is expected of them, i.e. what they need to do and how they should go about recording their results. Clear instructions should be provided and a response sheet made available to record results; or results can be recorded on a computer.
- Check that all tasters can taste the foods – i.e. there are no allergies, no smokers, no religious reasons why foods should be avoided, no-one tasting when they are feeling unwell, no-one wearing perfume/aftershave.
- Provide individual booths so that tasters aren't influenced or distracted by others. Make sure there is good lighting so they can clearly see the food sample(s).
- Samples should be the same size, served on the same dishes and coded randomly – either using random shapes like ●■♦✿ or random number combinations, e.g. 341, 47, 91, 183. Avoid using '1, 2, 3' or 'A, B, C', as these can often imply that '1' or 'A' is 'best'.
- Water and a dry cracker should be provided so that tasters can cleanse their palate in between tastings.
- Don't give tasters too many samples to taste, as their taste buds get tired and confused, and the results produced will not be as accurate. Test no more than six products at a time.

When the tasters get the food sample(s) placed in front of them, they will use **organoleptic factors,** meaning that they will be using different sense organs to assess such characteristics as:

- appearance
- taste or flavour
- texture (mouthfeel)
- smell or aroma.

APPEARANCE

The way food looks, in terms of colour and shape, will have an immediate effect on what tasters think about the product. Appearance can help to form opinions about the quality of the food: for example, a green banana tells you it is under-ripe, whereas fluffy mould growing on a tomato tells you it is no longer fit to eat.

Some sensory descriptors for appearance include: shiny, risen, colourful, dull, flat, cloudy, mottled.

TASTE OR FLAVOUR

There are about 10 000 taste buds located on the tongue, with children having more taste buds than adults. The four basic taste sensations that the tongue registers are: bitter, sour, salty and sweet.

Your tongue and the roof of your mouth are covered with thousands of tiny taste buds. When you eat something, the saliva in your mouth helps to break down your food. This causes the receptor cells located in your taste buds to send messages through sensory nerves to your brain. Your brain then tells you what flavours you are tasting.

Everyone's tastes are different. In fact, tastes often change with age. Babies have taste buds not only on their tongue but also on the sides and roof of their mouth. This means they are very sensitive to different foods. As they grow, the taste buds began to disappear from the sides and roof of the mouth, leaving taste buds mostly on the tongue. As people get older, taste buds become even less sensitive, so they will be more likely to eat foods thought as a child to be too strong.

Some sensory descriptors for taste include: spicy, sickly, treacly, sour, burnt, acidic, piquant, sweet, tangy.

TEXTURE OR MOUTHFEEL

Texture refers to the way food feels in the mouth; or it could be experienced by touching the food. It is not only the sense of feeling in the mouth, or 'mouthfeel', that is used; other senses too are involved to evaluate the texture of foods.

We make decisions about foods before we actually eat them. The ripeness of a pear is best judged by feeling it in our hands – gently squeezing it will tell us if it's ready to eat that day or not until a few days later. The colour of many fruits indicates their texture – green bananas will be too hard to eat, but brown ones will be mushy! When we do actually eat the food, we also use the sense of hearing; for example, the crunch of crisps.

Some sensory descriptors for texture include: creamy, gritty, slimy, crunchy, soggy, runny, crumbly, flaky, lumpy, smooth.

SMELL OR AROMA

The sense of smell is said to be about 10 000 times more sensitive than the sense of taste. Receptors are located in the nose and convey the sense of smell via the nasal passages to the brain.

Some sensory descriptors for smell include: pungent, burnt, stale, fruity, peppery, garlicky, sour.

ONLINE

Click onto Umami (www. brightredbooks.net/N5HFT) to find out what 'umami' is. As a follow-up activity, undertake the following product-development task – *Develop a umami-flavoured vegetable dish.*

VIDEO LINK

Visit the BrightRED Digital Zone to view clips on sensation and perception relating to the sense of sight, taste and smell.

ONLINE TEST

For a quiz on sensory testing, visit www.brightredbooks. net/N5HFT

THINGS TO DO AND THINK ABOUT

Look at the following BBC news article.

| Heinz to launch green ketchup | *Tuesday, 11 July, 2000, 15:21 GMT 16:21 UK* |

Food giant Heinz is launching a green-coloured version of one of its most famous products – tomato ketchup.

The staple of thousands of British dinner tables is as famous for its bright red appearance as it is for taking an age to pour from the bottle. But in a bid to capture more of the younger market, the American firm will bring in a spinach-coloured version of the classic sauce in the US this October.

As of January 2006, this product had been discontinued. Discuss why you think Heinz's new green ketchup was not a success.

TYPES OF SENSORY TESTS

PREFERENCE TESTS

These types of tests supply information about people's likes and dislikes of a product. They are subjective – i.e. you are asking here for an opinion, and what one person likes isn't necessarily the same as someone else. Preference tests are not designed to evaluate specific characteristics, so would not be used to find out how smooth or salty or colourful someone found a product.

Examples of a preference test: Ranking Test, Rating Test, Paired Comparison Test.

Ranking test

1. Decide on the products or characteristic of the products to be ranked, e.g. sweetness.

2. The tasters should taste each sample and place them in order in relation to how much or how little they like them or feel they have of the characteristic being asked about, e.g. 1 = favourite, down to 5 = like least, or 1 = very sweet, to 5 = not sweet at all.

3. The tasters' responses should be noted.

Rating test

1. Products, or specific characteristics of products, are tasted and then scored, e.g. on a 5-point scale where 1 = like very much, 2 = like, 3 = neutral, 4 = dislike and 5 = dislike a lot. Alternatively, smiley faces can be used instead:

....

2. The tasters' responses should be noted.

Paired comparison test (preference)

1. Tasters are asked to taste two samples.

2. They are asked which dish (or characteristic) they prefer.

3. The tasters' responses should be noted.

DISCRIMINATION TESTS

These types of tests aim to evaluate specific attributes of a product. They are objective, i.e. not influenced by personal feelings.

Examples of discrimination tests are a paired comparison test (discrimination) and a triangle test.

Paired comparison test (discrimination)

1. Tasters are asked to taste two samples.

2. They are asked to compare one characteristic or attribute: e.g. 'which one is crunchier?'

3. The tasters' responses should be noted.

ONLINE

Look at the example of a ranking test in the BrightRED Digital Zone.

ONLINE

Look at the examples of rating tests: www.brightredbooks.net/N5HFT

ONLINE

Look at the examples of paired comparison (preference) tests: www.brightredbooks.net/N5HFT

ONLINE

Look at the example of a paired comparison (discrimination) test on the BrightRED Digital Zone.

Triangle test

1 Three samples of food need to be prepared (they should look identical if possible). Two samples should be the same, and one should be different.

2 The three samples should be labelled and arranged in the shape of a triangle.

3 Tasters are asked to taste each sample in turn before deciding which of the samples is the odd one out.

4 The tasters' responses should be noted.

ONLINE

Look at the examples of triangle tests: www. brightredbooks.net/N5HFT

PROFILING TEST

This type of test allows the intensity of the sensory characteristic to be tasted and recorded – usually on a star chart or diagram.

1 Choose a number of attributes or sensory characteristics of the product(s) that you want to find out about.

2 Tasters are asked to taste the food sample(s) in turn and to decide on the intensity (using a scale from 0 to 5, where 0 = low and 5 = high intensity).

3 The tasters' responses should be noted on the star diagram.

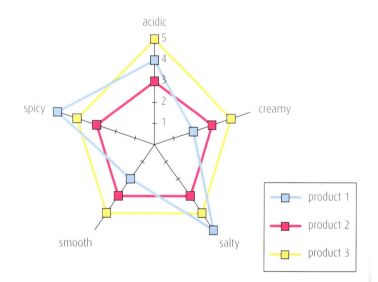

THINGS TO DO AND THINK ABOUT

You should carry out sensory testing of a food product you have made. You need to decide whom you will ask to taste your product, what method of testing you will use and how you will go about recording the results. You will also need to interpret the results and come to a conclusion about what you have found out.

For example, if you were to interpret the results of the testing of these three savoury risotto dishes, you might note a conclusion such as:

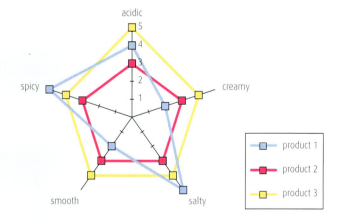

☺ Product 1 tasted nice and spicy, which I enjoyed, although this might not suit everyone; but it also scored high for salty. I would change this by adding herbs instead of salt to make the dish healthier.

☹ Product 3 tasted too acidic, but it had a lovely smooth and creamy texture, showing I had cooked the rice well and wouldn't need to change how long it was cooked for.

DON'T FORGET

You can use a star diagram to compare the same sensory attributes of more than one product. This may be useful when undertaking testing as part of your product-development coursework.

ONLINE

Look at the examples of profiling tests on the BrightRED Digital Zone.

ONLINE TEST

Check how well you have learned about sensory testing online at www. brightredbooks.net/N5HFT

FACTORS AFFECTING CONSUMERS' CHOICE OF FOOD 1

Consumers have a complex relationship with food, driven by such factors as:

- biological factors
- environmental factors
- social factors
- economic factors
- cultural and religious factors
- nutritional and dietary factors.

You will be required to *explain* factors which may affect consumers' choice of food. For now, let us consider how biological and economic factors can affect consumers' choice of food.

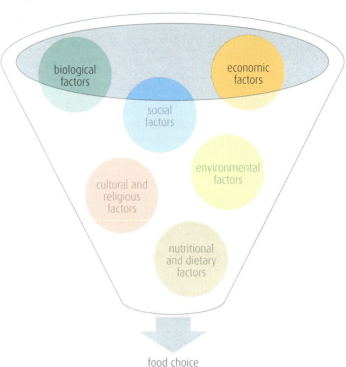

food choice

BIOLOGICAL FACTORS

Hunger/satiety

The main reason people eat is because they are hungry – but *what* they choose to eat isn't necessarily determined by their nutritional needs. Everyone needs energy and nutrients to survive; and the body will respond to, and control, the balance between hunger and satiety.

Satiety is when the body feels full after eating.

Likes/dislikes

How pleasing people find particular foods is often referred to as 'palatability'. The taste, smell, appearance and texture of food all add to its palatability. Some people are adventurous and like to try new foods, while others stick to what they are familiar with and know they like. The food industry produces a huge choice of food products to suit a wide variety of tastes, thus offering more variety in the diet.

Age

Choice of food, and food needs, vary depending upon the stage of life people are at. For example, babies' food should not contain salt, as it is dangerous because their kidneys are not able to process large amounts of salt. Toddlers should not be given low-fat foods on a regular basis, as they need fat in their diet to ensure they get the necessary fat-soluble vitamins. Elderly people should aim to eat nutrient-rich foods but avoid high-calorie options, as they may not be active, so any excess energy consumed will be stored as body fat.

ENVIRONMENTAL FACTORS

Climate

Climate and weather conditions affect the types of food that can be grown in the country. For example, Scotland grows soft fruit and root vegetables in our rainy/ temperate climate, whereas pineapples and bananas need a warm climate to grow.

- When the weather is cold, people may opt for foods that provide warmth, such as soup. The opposite is the case in summer, when salads and fruit may be more popular.

- Greater knowledge of factors such as **food miles** may mean that people are now more aware of how far their food has travelled and may mean they choose locally grown produce instead.

- Environmentally friendly products are often bought by people because they feel these reflect their views about food.

Organic

Some consumers choose to purchase food that has been grown without the use of man-made chemicals and fertilisers because they may have concerns that such chemicals could have cancer-causing properties.

- People may buy organic foods in the belief that these taste better and contain higher levels of certain nutrients.

Carbon footprint

This refers to the amount of CO_2 and other greenhouse gases emitted over the life cycle of a product. Some consumers choose to buy food products with a low carbon footprint because they are concerned about the environment.

Food miles

This refers to the distance food travels from field to plate and the impact made by transporting food around the world. In the past, fruit and vegetables were eaten only when they were in season locally; however, consumers now have the choice to eat what they want all year round.

Animal cruelty

Many consumers are concerned about how animals are bred and treated within the food chain – and this can influence the products they buy.

Many people opt for free-range as opposed to battery eggs and chickens if they are not comfortable with the hens being kept indoors in cages, preferring instead for them to be allowed to roam free.

Many customers choose only fish products that bear the MSC (Marine Stewardship Council) label to show that it comes from a sustainable source.

Consumers may opt to buy tinned tuna with a dolphin-friendly logo on it, as they can then be assured that the design of the net and method of catching the tuna will not have caused harm to dolphins.

THINGS TO DO AND THINK ABOUT

Undertake some research into the issue of fish being discarded into the sea (http://www. fishfight.net/). Use your research to produce a poster to highlight the issues raised by this campaign.

Consider the factors that go to make up a good poster – e.g. informative, clear to read, colourful/eye-catching. Undertake a peer evaluation of the posters. Provide feedback.

VIDEO LINK

Watch the clip on how one family tried to reduce their carbon footprint at the BrightRED Digital Zone.

ONLINE TEST

How well do you know about the biological and environmental factors that can affect consumers' choice of food? Test yourself online at www.brightredbooks.net/ N5HFT

FACTORS AFFECTING CONSUMERS' CHOICE OF FOOD 2

SOCIAL FACTORS

Family

Family is an important social influence upon food choice. Often, food is eaten because it has been served up to the family at mealtimes.

- Changes to family structures may mean fewer shared mealtimes and more snacking.

- The increase in the number of parents working may mean that more convenience and takeaway meals are purchased/eaten, as they take less time to prepare/cook.

- More people now live alone and may choose one-portion meals to avoid waste.

Lifestyle

Leading busier lifestyles has resulted in an increase in pre-prepared ingredients such as jars of sauces and ready-prepared vegetables.

- Greater use of labour-saving food preparation and cooking equipment such as blenders, microwaves and healthy grills reduces the amount of time needed to be spent on food preparation, therefore affects the ingredients/products chosen.

- There has been an increase in the number of people opting to eat out at restaurants, thus increasing the choice of food available.

- There is a greater number of takeaway food/drink outlets, giving consumers greater choice and the convenience of no preparation required.

- Loss of practical cookery skills has resulted in fewer people preparing meals from scratch, and more reliance on pre-prepared/convenience foods.

Peers

Our food choice can depend on other people. Adolescents are often influenced by where and what their friends eat in order to gain the acceptance of the peer group.

- The venue in which food is eaten can affect food choice, particularly in terms of what foods are on offer. For example, the school canteen meals have to follow nutritional guidelines that may result in healthy food options that teenagers don't want, therefore they may opt instead to go to local outlets selling high-fat/sugar foods.

Occupation

People who have sedentary jobs, e.g. office workers, may need to choose to consume foods that have a lower fat/energy content, as they may not burn off the excess calories and thus will store them as body fat, increasing their risk of obesity. The opposite may be true of those who are doing manual/physical work, such as builders.

- Those who work shifts have irregular eating patterns, and may mean people in a household all eating at different times. This could increase the amount of ready meals eaten, as these are quick to heat whenever people get home from work.

- Many people opt to eat at their desks at work, choosing handy-to-eat prepared sandwiches or snacks, as opposed to taking time out to sit and have a meal at lunchtime.

Advertising and media

Media has a major influence on food choice. Advertisements promote food products and can show consumers what is available, but they can also persuade people to buy products that they don't necessarily need or that may not be good for their health.

contd

- Primary products, such as milk, meat, fruit and vegetables, tend not to be advertised; however, if they were, it may have an influence on people's healthy food choices and lead to an improvement in diet.

- UK regulations ban the advertising of foods high in fat, salt or sugar during children's TV programmes, as it was felt that exposure to such advertising increased 'pester power', where children were influencing the types of products parents purchased when out shopping for food.

- Ways of promoting products vary depending upon the target group: for example, free toys may be given out with children's food products to encourage them to repeat-purchase.

- Advertising aims to influence consumers' brand choice so that manufacturers can be confident their customers will return time and time again to purchase the same brand.

ECONOMIC FACTORS

Cost/budget

The amount of money people have to spend on food, and how much the food costs, will influence the quantity, quality and variety of food that can be bought.

- Cheaper cuts of meat, like sausages, may be higher in fat whereas leaner cuts, such as fillet steak, tend to be more expensive.

- Fresh fruit and vegetables may sometimes not be purchased for fear of waste.

- Sometimes ready meals can cost less than the total cost of buying ingredients separately, and these may not be the healthiest option.

- Food from a cheaper value range may be lower in nutritional value or higher in fat/sugar/salt than, for example, fresh organic food.

Accessibility

Access to transport may mean that the choice of food is limited to what's available in a local shop, or it may affect what a shopper can carry home.

- A local shop may offer convenience, but might have limited choice and cost more.

- 24-hour supermarket opening means that consumers can choose to shop when it suits them, and it gives them a wide range of products to choose from.

- Internet shopping allows those who cannot gain access to a shop the ability to choose whatever they want and to have the goods delivered to their home whenever they want, though at an extra cost.

Foreign travel

The increase in foreign travel has resulted in a growth in the range and types of foreign food now available to buy in the UK.

- When people travel abroad, and taste different foods, they are keen to have the opportunity to sample similar foods when they get home, so manufacturers have picked up on this and now offer a wide range of ethnic ingredients and dishes.

- The UK has a diverse population, which has greatly influenced the choice of food available from takeaway outlets.

THINGS TO DO AND THINK ABOUT

Experiment with producing and comparing fresh and convenience foods. Reflect upon your results in terms of preparation time, cost, nutritional value, shelf life and taste.

VIDEO LINK

More information on this can be found via watching the clip 'Branding – Building the Value': www.brightredbooks.net/N5HFT

DON'T FORGET

Each of these comments provides an explanation as to why/how the factor affects consumers' choices – and this is what you will need to do to pass the assessment for this unit.

ONLINE TEST

How well do you know about the social and economic factors that can affect consumers' choice of food? Test yourself online at www.brightredbooks.net/N5HFT

FACTORS AFFECTING CONSUMERS' CHOICE OF FOOD 3

So, we have now explored the biological, economical, social and environmental affecting consumers' food choice. Let's have a look at the other factors: cultural and religious, and nutritional and dietary.

CULTURAL/RELIGIOUS FACTORS

Many cultures and religions have dietary rules which affect the food choices people can make.

Religion	Food choices
Christianity	Christian religion does not forbid eating any foods; however, some Catholics may choose to eat fish on a Friday instead of meat. Christmas is a Christian festival to celebrate the birth of Jesus; and special food may be served at this time. At Easter time, some Christians may choose to decorate or roll eggs to represent the boulder being rolled from the tomb at the time of the resurrection.
Islam	Food must be halal, which means that animals are slaughtered according to Muslim law. Pork is forbidden, as are fish without scales, shellfish and alcohol. Muslims celebrate Ramadan, and fasting takes place during that month. The end of Ramadan is celebrated, and sugared almonds and sweets are exchanged as gifts. Alcohol is forbidden because the Qur'an states that intoxication of any kind leads to forgetfulness of prayer and of God.
Hinduism	For Hindus, the cow is sacred, as are its products such as milk and ghee, therefore they are not eaten. Many Hindus are vegetarian, but some eat meat. The exception is that pig meat (pork) and shellfish are considered unclean and so are not eaten.
Judaism	Jewish people only eat kosher meats, which means the meat is slaughtered and prepared to strict Jewish laws. Forbidden foods include pork, bacon, ham, shellfish, eels and gelatine. Meat must not be cooked with butter; and milk and meat should not be cooked together or eaten together. The Feast of the Passover is celebrated by Jewish people.
Sikhism	Food restrictions for Sikhs are less strict than for some other religions; however, beef is forbidden, as is alcohol.

NUTRITIONAL/DIETARY FACTORS

Consumers' choice of food can be linked to diet-related conditions or to food allergies/intolerances, or to how much people know about the ways in which food can affect their health.

contd

VIDEO LINK

Have a look at the clip about fasting during Ramadan at www.brightredbooks.net/N5HFT

VIDEO LINK

Have a look at the clip about the Seder meal: www.brightredbooks.net/N5HFT

VIDEO LINK

For more, head to the BrightRED Digital Zone and check out the clip about Sikh food.

Nutritional knowledge

There is increased awareness of the nutritional content of food, which should allow consumers to choose healthier options.

Initiatives, such as front-of-pack labelling/traffic-lighting, alert consumers as to the fat/salt/sugar content of the products they might choose.

Some consumers may be confused by the range of information on labels, so may find it difficult to make informed choices.

There are many low-fat, low-salt, low-sugar products available for consumers who are keen to choose healthier options.

Health

Some people may have different dietary needs depending upon the stage that they are at in their life and their overall health.

A diet high in fat/salt/sugar may increase the risk of people suffering dietary diseases such as hypertension, coronary heart disease and obesity.

Allergies may affect choice. For example, some people may be allergic to peanuts or to gluten in wheat, so have to avoid these ingredients when choosing foods so as to prevent allergic reactions occurring.

Some people opt to follow a vegetarian diet, as they believe that consuming only foods from plant sources is healthier than eating meat and animal products.

DON'T FORGET

At National 5 level, you have to **identify** and **explain** a minimum of **three** factors that affect consumers' choice of food.

ONLINE TEST

How well do you know about cultural/religious and nutritional/dietary factors which can affect consumers' choice of food? Test yourself online at www.brightredbooks.net/N5HFT

THINGS TO DO AND THINK ABOUT

- Look at the data from the Scottish Government's 2012 Healthy Living Survey on the uptake of school meals: http://www.scotland.gov.uk/Publications/2012/06/4917/6. Discuss why you think it is that the number of pupils eating school meals at secondary school is consistently lower than the number who eat school meals in primary school. Undertake a survey seeking classmates' views on your school canteen. Find out what are the main factors that affect whether or not pupils choose to eat in the canteen.

- Watch this short video clip on how culture and society shape our views on food: http://www.bbc.co.uk/learningzone/clips/how-culture-and-society-shape-our-views-of-food/8570.html. Investigate kosher and halal food: http://www.koshercertification.org.uk/whatdoe.html; http://www.halalfoodauthority.com/

- Undertake some research to find unleavened bread recipes that could be served at Passover. Design and make your own version of unleavened bread.

- Produce a food product which would be suitable for someone whose food choices are influenced by their religion.

ISSUES AFFECTING CONSUMERS' CHOICE OF FOOD 1

This topic is all about developing knowledge and understanding of a range of current contemporary food issues. These issues may be topical and subject to change over time. Current issues that affect consumers' food choices include:

- allotments/grow-your-own initiatives
- factory farming
- Fairtrade
- food/air miles
- food advertising/labelling
- food aid/world hunger
- food co-operatives
- organic produce
- pollution/recycling
- seasonality
- sustainability.

You will be required to *explain* how at least *three* contemporary food issues may affect consumers' choice of food. For now, let's look more closely at allotments/grow-your-own initiatives, factory farming and Fairtrade.

ALLOTMENTS/GROW-YOUR-OWN INITIATIVES

```
                    Less contact with pesticides
                    if grown organically, so
                    perceived health benefits

Research has shown that                      Can expand range of fruit
involvement in allotments                    and vegetables eaten via
increases consumption of                     growing a wide/diverse
fruit and vegetables                         range of produce

              ALLOTMENTS/GROW-YOUR-OWN INITIATIVES

Less or no packaging                                 A sustainable food source


    Can be picked and eaten                      Growers feel they
    fresh, therefore less likely                 are benefiting the
    to have suffered loss of      Money-saving    environment/minimal
    water-soluble vitamins                        carbon footprint
```

FACTORY FARMING

Key points:

- Consumers may decide against buying factory-farmed meat due to taste, as organically reared animals generally take longer to fatten, thus producing better-tasting meat

contd

- Consumers may reject factory-farmed foods for ethical reasons: they consider animals to be treated cruelly

- There is potential for an increase in diseases such as salmonella when large numbers of animals are kept together indoors, which customers would want to avoid for health reasons

- Consumers may avoid buying factory-farmed foods due to having serious health concerns around the build-up of potential resistance via the over-use of antibiotics

- Consumers might choose to buy factory-farmed food for cost reasons, as it may be cheaper to buy if they are on a budget

- Because of concerns about factory farming, consumers may opt instead to follow a vegetarian diet

- Consumers might reject choosing factory-farmed foods if they are concerned about the smell and potential pollution that such factories may produce.

FAIRTRADE

Fairtrade ensures disadvantaged farmers and workers in developing countries get a better deal. By meeting Fairtrade standards, businesses are able to put the FAIRTRADE Mark on products. Through Fairtrade, farmers and workers in developed countries receive a fair and stable price as well as the Fairtrade premium, which they choose to invest in their communities and businesses for a sustainable future. There are currently over 3000 Fairtrade products certified in the UK, from tea and coffee through to flowers and cotton.

Key points:

- Consumers may decide against choosing Fairtrade products, as these can sometimes be more expensive to buy than similar goods

- Consumers may feel it is important to support workers in developing countries, so they would be keen to support this via choosing to buy Fairtrade products

- Not all stores stock Fairtrade products, and those that do may not have a vast range on offer, thus limiting consumers' choices

- In some cases, Fairtrade products are grown organically, which attracts consumers to buy them as they consider them to be kind to the environment

- Some consumers choose Fairtrade products as they consider them to be good quality because of how they are grown.

 ## THINGS TO DO AND THINK ABOUT

Investigate the range of Fairtrade products on offer that you could use to make some banana muffins. Undertake a costing exercise to work out the cost of a batch of Fairtrade banana muffins versus using non-Fairtrade ingredients. Produce both batches of banana muffins. Carry out sensory evaluation after making both batches. Reflect on your results – which do you prefer, and why?

 VIDEO LINK

Watch the clip entitled 'Why is factory farming such a big deal?' at www.brightredbooks.net/N5HFT

 DON'T FORGET

There are two sides to every story. Why not undertake some research into the issue of factory farming and carry out a class debate on the key issues?

 ONLINE

Why not see how much you know about Fairtrade by trying the quiz? (www.brightredbooks.net/N5HFT)

 VIDEO LINK

Go to the BrightRED Digital Zone and watch the short film which documents two Fairtrade-certified banana producers in the Dominican Republic.

 ONLINE TEST

How well do you know about current issues that affect consumers' food choices? Test yourself online at www.brightredbooks.net/N5HFT

ISSUES AFFECTING CONSUMERS' CHOICE OF FOOD 2

Now let's have a look at how the issues of food/air miles, food advertising/labelling and food aid/world hunger can affect consumers' choice of food.

VIDEO LINK

Watch the video clip on food miles and wastage in the UK: www.brightredbooks.net/N5HFT. Think about the list of the top foods it mentions we waste. Choose one of these foods, and develop a dish containing this ingredient.

FOOD/AIR MILES

Food miles means the distance that food travels from where it is grown to where it is bought – sometimes referred to as 'from field to plate'. This is an environmental concern to some consumers because of the CO_2 emissions from transport.

Carbon footprint for food is the total amount of CO_2 and other greenhouse gases emitted over the life cycle of a product.

Key points:

- Some consumers don't mind how far a food has travelled as long as they can choose what they want throughout the year.

- Some consumers question if food miles really matter, as you can use at least as much energy heating a greenhouse to grow produce in the UK as you can growing it outside in a warm climate and flying it to the UK.

- To some consumers, climate change is an important issue and they would be looking to choose foods that have a low carbon footprint.

- Supporting local suppliers/farmers by buying locally grown foods is something some consumers will do in order to reduce the environmental impact of importing goods.

- Depending upon how far the food has travelled, and how long it takes to reach the consumer, it may have lost some nutritional content, which will put some consumers off buying the food.

VIDEO LINK

Head to the BrightRED Digital Zone to watch the TV ad from the 1970s that was voted one of the best of all time. Its aim was to persuade consumers to buy this convenience food, as opposed to preparing fresh potato. Investigate the ingredients and nutritional value of Smash versus fresh potato. Produce a potato-based pie using both, and undertake sensory evaluation. Reflect on your findings.

FOOD ADVERTISING/LABELLING

Food advertising has, over the years, been accused of increasing UK obesity rates due to the number of adverts for fast food which is high in fat/sugar/salt, influencing consumers to want to buy such products.

In order to protect consumers, an EU regulation came into force in July 2007 controlling what advertisers could say about health and nutritional claims relating to food products.

TV adverts

Advertisements for unhealthy foods are not allowed to be shown on children's TV channels, with the aim of trying to prevent children's food choices from being influenced by ads for high-fat/sugar/salt foods they see on TV.

contd

Some advertisers are trying to get around the TV ban by using the internet. For example, Cheestrings by Kerry Foods falls foul of the TV ban because each portion contains a third more salt than the average bag of crisps, but their website targets children with fun games that encourage them to become familiar with, and want to have, the product. What do you think about this practice? Discuss with your classmates.

ONLINE

Check out the Cheestrings link at www.brightredbooks. net/N5HFT

FOOD AID/WORLD HUNGER

There are 870 million **undernourished** people in the world today. That means one in eight people do not get enough food to be healthy and lead an active life.

Key points:

- Some consumers may decide to buy and donate food to give to food-aid initiatives, such as the UN World Food Programme.

- Consumers may opt to boycott food from certain organisations or countries if they feel that these act in an unethical way.

- People living in poverty may have access to 'surplus' food that is distributed by charities. Such food may be close to, or on, its use-by date but will be a source of nutrition that would otherwise be unavailable to them.

- More children now than ever access breakfast clubs in school as a means of getting food to start their day – food that they otherwise would not have got at home.

THINGS TO DO AND THINK ABOUT

1 Undertake internet research to investigate the range of fruit and vegetables on offer. Look at where they come from. You could plot these on a map to highlight the distance they have travelled to get to Scotland.

2 It's not just people in Africa who suffer from malnutrition – people in Scotland may not be getting the nutrients they need from their diet to keep them healthy. Why might this be the case? Undertake some research into the links between junk-food diets and malnutrition.

DON'T FORGET

Remember to check pages 80–83 to get further in-depth information on how information on food labels helps consumers to make informed choices.

ONLINE

The hunger map link will let you see a map showing the areas of the world at greatest risk of suffering from hunger: www. brightredbooks.net/N5HFT

ONLINE TEST

How well do you know about current issues that affect consumers' food choices? Test yourself online at www. brightredbooks.net/N5HFT

ISSUES AFFECTING CONSUMERS' CHOICE OF FOOD 3

Some further contemporary food issues which affect consumers' choice of food and which we will now investigate are food co-operatives, organic produce and pollution/recycling.

FOOD CO-OPERATIVES

The main principle behind all community-run food co-ops is that, by pooling their buying power and ordering food in bulk direct from suppliers, a group of people can buy good food at a more affordable price.

Key points:

- Consumers who buy their food through a co-op do so at a more affordable price.

- They have more control over where their food comes from, which may be important to some consumers.

- A food co-op operating in a local area allows consumers to gain access to food that might otherwise be unavailable to them if they live in a remote area.

- To some consumers, it is important that they support local providers, as opposed to shopping at large supermarkets.

- Food co-ops may offer consumers the choice of unusual produce that other shops do not stock.

- Food from a co-op may have less packaging and less waste, thus is a more environmentally friendly option for consumers who consider this to be an important issue.

VIDEO LINK

Watch the food co-operative UK video at www.brightredbooks.net/N5HFT

ORGANIC PRODUCE

Organic food is produced using environmentally and animal-friendly farming methods. For foods to be labelled as organic, *at least 95%* of the ingredients must come from organically produced plants and animals, and it must have been produced to EU regulations and inspected and certified by a registered certification body, such as the Soil Association.

Key points:

- Many consumers choose organic food because they believe it tastes better.

- Some consumers believe organic food is better for their health as it has been grown without the use of chemicals and artificial fertilisers.

- If a consumer is concerned about environmental issues, they may opt to buy organic produce, as this method of growing food is kinder to the planet.

- Nature-loving consumers may choose organic food, as organic farming encourages wildlife.

ONLINE

Click on the Soil Association link in the BrightRED Digital Zone to find out more about information on a food label that relates to a product advertised as being organic.

contd

- People who are concerned about the welfare of animals choose organic food as organic standards insist that animals are given plenty of space and fresh air to thrive and grow – guaranteeing a truly free-range life.

- Due to organic farming being more labour-intensive than other farming, it can mean higher costs for foods, which not all consumers can afford.

- There is no clear scientific evidence that organically farmed-food is healthier than non-organic produce. However, organic standards do not allow hydrogenated fats and controversial addities like aspartame, tartazine and MSG.

POLLUTION/RECYCLING

Scottish households throw away 566 000 tonnes of food waste every year. Over two thirds of this could be avoided if it were more effectively planned, stored and managed. Avoidable food waste costs Scotland nearly £1 billion – that's the equivalent of £430 per household! Wasted food is not only a waste of money; it's also a major contributor to climate change. Producing, transporting and storing food uses a lot of energy, water and packaging, which is all wasted if the food gets thrown away uneaten. If this avoidable food waste had been consumed, it would prevent the equivalent of 1.7 million tonnes of carbon dioxide entering the atmosphere – roughly the same as taking one in every five cars off Scotland's roads.

DON'T FORGET

You should try to compost as much of your food waste as possible. Check if your local authority issues food-waste caddies for this purpose.

Key points:

- Some consumers may choose to buy food from a local farmers' market or a food co-operative so that there is reduced/no packaging, thus preventing waste going to landfill.

- Increased awareness of recycling means that consumers are able to check products' packaging to identify the symbols that state if it is able to be recycled or not.

- Consumers might decide to buy in bulk, as larger packs tend to have less packaging than smaller ones.

- Consumers may choose to cut down on food waste/putting food to landfill via using up or freezing leftovers.

ONLINE TEST

How well do you know about current issues that affect consumers' food choices? Test yourself online at www.brightredbooks.net/N5HFT

THINGS TO DO AND THINK ABOUT

Produce a questionnaire which contains between 5 and 8 questions that will allow you to find out more about your friends' and family's awareness of recycling and what measures they currently use to be environmentally friendly and avoid food waste. Evaluate your results. Discuss with your classmates. Is the overall picture for recycling and food waste positive or negative? Is there anything you could do about it?

ISSUES AFFECTING CONSUMERS' CHOICE OF FOOD 4

Finally, let's have a look at seasonality and sustainability.

SEASONALITY

Seasonality refers to the time of year when the food is at its very best, either in terms of flavour or when it is harvested to be at its freshest.

Key points:

- Local seasonal food tends to be fresher and cheaper, as there is less transportation time/cost involved

- Foods are usually harvested when they are at their peak, so are considered by some consumers to have the most flavour and nutrients

- Due to the lack of transport from field to fork, local produce in season is chosen by some consumers who are interested in environmental conservation

- Eating in season, and buying what consumers need locally, should help to prevent food waste

- Buying in season from local producers allows consumers to support the local economy

- Visiting 'pick-your-own' farms not only allows consumers to choose produce in season but can also be a fun family day out

- Buying seasonal food from a farmers' market allows consumers to speak to the producer to find out more about the products on sale, perhaps getting advice on recipes to try.

SUSTAINABILITY

This is all about endurance: making sure that there isn't only enough food for today but also that future supplies have been secured. Sustainable food should be produced, processed and traded in ways that contribute to thriving local economies, protect the diversity of both plants and animals (and the welfare of farmed and wild species) and avoid damaging natural resources or contributing to climate change.

Key points:

- Consumers may decide to avoid bottled water, and drink tap water instead, so as to limit the amount of packaging that goes into landfill

- Consumers may decide to avoid buying fish that is considered 'at risk', such as cod, which has been overfished, and instead buy seabass, which is considered sustainable

- Some consumers might not worry about over-fished supplies and continue to buy fish purely on the basis that they like to eat it or think it benefits their health, e.g. mackerel

- Buying food from local suppliers allows consumers to support the local economy so that the growers can continue to produce and sell their produce

- Animal farming causes high levels of greenhouse gas emissions, which may result in some consumers choosing to reduce the amount of red meat they eat or opting to become a vegetarian due to environmental and health concerns

contd

- Better availability of fresh, local sustainable foods may allow consumers to make healthier food choices, thus avoiding high-fat/sugar/salt-content convenience foods

- Some consumers might decide to start growing their own vegetables or keeping their own animals, such as hens, to provide them with food.

 THINGS TO DO AND THINK ABOUT

1 Look at this picture advertising eggs. Why do you think the caption 'Soldiering on' is used with this picture?

Investigate what the red lion stamp means on an egg.

Develop an egg dish that can be used to promote British eggs.

2 Case Study: Duchy Originals Organic Foods

HRH Prince Charles owns an organic farm called Duchy Home Farm. Read its story at http://www.duchyoriginals.com/our_story.php

Duchy's first product was an oaten biscuit. Their product-development team are keen to expand their range of organic oat-based biscuits. Your task is to develop a biscuit using oats that can be added to this classic range.

3 Devise a 60-second news segment linked to a contemporary food issue of your choice. You might want to film it as an advertisement. Get your classmates or teacher to give you some feedback.

 ONLINE

Look at the information on the Marine Conservation Society website: www.brightredbooks.net/N5HFT. Find a sustainable fish that you perhaps haven't tried before. Undertake some research into this fish before developing a dish using your chosen fish that would encourage others to try it.

 ONLINE

Try the video-link quiz to see how much you know about sustainability: www.brightredbooks.net/N5HFT

 ONLINE TEST

How well do you know about current issues that affect consumers' food choices? Test yourself online at www.brightredbooks.net/N5HFT

TECHNOLOGICAL DEVELOPMENTS AFFECTING CONSUMERS' CHOICE OF FOOD 1

This topic is all about developing knowledge and understanding of a range of current technological developments affecting food. New developments are being introduced all the time. Some current technological developments that impact upon consumers' food choices include:

- alternative proteins/meat analogues
- extrusion cooking
- food additives
- functional foods
- genetically modified foods
- hydroponics
- irradiation
- modified-atmosphere packaging
- nanotechnology
- smart ingredients
- ultra-high temperature/ultra-heat-treated (UHT)
- vacuum packing

Let's begin by looking at the technological developments in alternative proteins/meat analogues and extrusion cooking.

DON'T FORGET

You will be required to **explain** how at least **two** technological developments may affect consumers' choice of food.

ALTERNATIVE PROTEINS/MEAT ANALOGUES

Meat analogues are foods that are manufactured in such a way that they look, taste and can be used in similar ways to meat but are made from vegetable sources.

Quorn™

Quorn™ is a mycoprotein. It is a tiny mushroom-like fungus which grows very quickly in a glucose solution. After a few days, it is harvested, rolled into sheets and set by steaming. It is then able to be processed into shapes – minced, sliced, cubed.

Textured Vegetable Protein (TVP)

TVP is made from soya beans once the oil has been taken out. The remaining bean is ground into flour, mixed with water to form a dough and extruded to form chunks or shapes.

Tofu

Tofu is made from soya-bean curd, and forms a smooth-textured semi-solid white coloured block. It can be marinated to add more flavour.

Key points:

- Meat analogues are low in fat, therefore are useful for consumers wishing to follow a low-fat diet.

- Meat analogues tend to be bland but good at taking on flavourings added to them, offering consumers lots of variety in relation to what they add to it to provide flavour.

- Meat analogues are high in dietary fibre so may be attractive to consumers looking for a high-fibre option.

- Quorn may not be a suitable choice for vegans, as egg-white is often used in the manufacturing process.

- TVP is an excellent source of high biological value protein because it is derived from soya, which makes it ideal for vegetarians and vegans so they don't miss out on any essential amino acids.

DON'T FORGET

Soya bean is the only vegetable source to have a high biological value (HBV) and contain all essential amino acids required for growth in children.

contd.

- Meat analogues provide consumers with a less expensive form of protein, so may be chosen by consumers on a budget to save money.

- TVP can be dried, allowing consumers to store it in a cupboard for long periods of time, thus providing them with a convenient product that could be handy in emergencies.

EXTRUSION COOKING

Extrusion was first used in the snack industry back in the 1930s, with the production of corn curl crisps (Quavers). Raw ingredients are placed into a hopper. The screw is rotated, forcing materials along the barrel. Heat may be applied or removed, depending on the product. The product emerges through a die, formed into the desired shape. Typically, extruded foods have a high starch content.

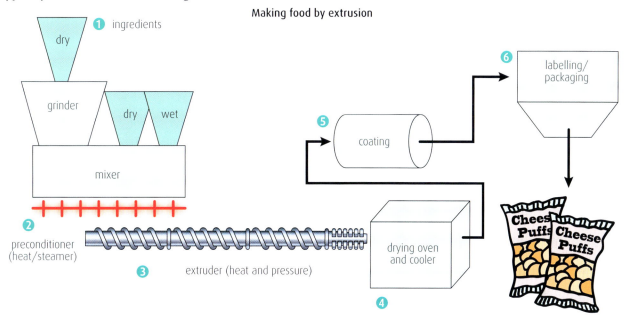

Making food by extrusion

Key points:

- A wide variety of snacks, including crisps like cheese puffs and onion rings, are produced from potato, corn or rice starch. This offers a variety of options – but they are usually deep-fried after extrusion, so are not a particularly healthy option.

- A broad range of breakfast cereals are produced using extrusion cooking. Once shaped, the cereals may be sugar-coated and toasted in an oven to give a crunchy texture.

- Often, cheaper raw materials are able to be used in extrusion cooking, so production costs are lower, which should result in better-value products for consumers.

- Extruding pasta allows manufacturers to offer consumers a huge range of shapes to choose from, giving variety in the diet.

- Extrusion enables mass-production of food via a continuous, efficient system that ensures uniformity of the final product so that consumers can be assured of consistency of the end product.

 VIDEO LINK

Want to view the extrusion process? Do so via watching the clip at www.brightredbooks.net/N5HFT

 ONLINE TEST

Test yourself on meat alternatives and extrusion online at www.brightredbooks.net/N5HFT

 THINGS TO DO AND THINK ABOUT

Make a batch of spaghetti bolognese using a range of different meat analogues. Carry out sensory testing. Evaluate your results.

TECHNOLOGICAL DEVELOPMENTS AFFECTING CONSUMERS' CHOICE OF FOOD 2

Another technological development which has affected food choice is the development of food additives.

FOOD ADDITIVES

Additives are substances that are added to foods in small amounts during food processing to perform a specific function. There are over 300 listed additives and more than 3000 flavourings. Additives may be natural or artificial. The main groups of food additives are antioxidants, colours, flavour enhancers, sweeteners, emulsifiers, stabilisers and preservatives.

All additives are thoroughly assessed for safety before they are allowed to be used. Approved additives are given a number, and some are also given an 'E' if they've been accepted for safe use within the European Union.

Category of additive	E-numbers	Function
Flavourings/flavour enhancers		Used to add flavour to food, e.g. vanilla to ice cream, or to restore flavours lost during processing.
Colourings	E100–E199	Used to make food more attractive or to replace colour that may have been lost during processing. Caramel is the most popular colour, e.g. used in pickled onions. Some colours are also vitamins (e.g. riboflavin and beta-carotene); and there are only 3 colours allowed in baby food.
Preservatives	E200–E299	Used to increase storage life by preventing deterioration from micro-organisms, such as bacteria or mould. Traditional methods, such as using salt to cure meat, are still used to keep food safer to eat for longer.

contd

Antioxidants	E300–E321	These prevent foods containing fat from going rancid, and prevent fruit from oxidising/going brown, so extending shelf life.
Emulsifiers and stabilisers	E322–E499	These are used to help substances such as oil and water mix together, e.g. salad dressing. They give foods a smooth, creamy texture and can extend shelf life. Lecithin is a natural emulsion found in eggs and is used in the making of mayonnaise.
Sweeteners	E500 upwards	There are two types of sweeteners: intense and bulk. Intense sweeteners, e.g. saccharin or aspartame, are respectively 300 and 2000 times sweeter than sucrose. Bulk sweeteners, e.g. sorbitol, are used in the same quantities as sugar.
Other additives		Raising agents, e.g. sodium bicarbonate, are used to give a lighter texture to baked products. Thickening agents are used to form a gel to thicken sauces. Propellants are used in sprays such as squirty cream.

Key points:

- An increasing number of consumers want to buy 'natural' food products because they have concerns about certain chemicals being added to their food, and feel there is an increased risk to health, therefore they may choose to buy organic food instead.

- If manufacturers meet consumer demands for fewer additives, it will mean a shortened shelf life for their products and could cost the consumer more to buy.

- Consumers may not choose products if they contain no additives, especially colouring if the food had lost colour during processing and looks unappealing.

- Some parents choose to avoid foods that contain certain colourings, as they feel there is a link to hyperactivity in children.

- If a consumer is looking for a low-calorie option, they may choose a product that has artificial sweetener added to it, as this will provide them with low-energy options.

- The use of additives to fortify products, such as breakfast cereals, provides consumers with additional nutrients that are beneficial to health.

- The use of additives allows consumers to have products that are of a consistent quality.

- The use of additives in food manufacturing allows producers to offer consumers products with a wide range of flavours, e.g. smoky-bacon or sour-cream-and-chive flavour crisps.

ONLINE

Check out the 'Understanding Food Additives' link in the BrightRED Digital Zone to read more.

ONLINE TEST

Test yourself on food additives at www.brightredbooks.net/N5HFT

DON'T FORGET

'Fortification' is the process of adding nutrients to food, e.g. adding folic acid to flour.

THINGS TO DO AND THINK ABOUT

Have a look at this newspaper article, entitled 'Should we be fortifying foods with nutrients?': http://www.independent.co.uk/life-style/food-and-drink/features/should-we-be-fortifying-foods-with-nutrients-6348759.html. Produce a presentation that explains the advantages and disadvantages of using additives in foods.

TECHNOLOGICAL DEVELOPMENTS AFFECTING CONSUMERS' CHOICE OF FOOD 3

Now let's consider functional foods, genetically modified foods and hydroponics and their effect on consumers' food choice.

DON'T FORGET

'Superfoods': there is actually no specific definition of a superfood and no way of testing whether a food is 'super' or not. The term is sometimes used to describe a food that is rich in a particular nutrient or other bioactive substance, e.g. tomato products containing lycopene (linked to the reduction of prostate cancer), or cranberries containing tannins that improve urinary-tract health.

FUNCTIONAL FOODS

In addition to being nutritious, functional foods offer additional health benefits over their basic nutritional value. For example, probiotics/prebiotics added to yoghurt/drinks top up good bacteria in the gut; stanols/sterols added to margarine can help lower cholesterol levels; omega 3 fatty acids are added to milk.

Key points:

- Functional foods can provide consumers with a more concentrated form of a specific substance than they might get from consuming a normal diet.

- Consumers who have an allergy to seafood may benefit from eating functional foods which have been fortified with omega 3 fatty acids, such as egg.

- Functional foods have the potential to improve health and reduce the risk of certain dietary conditions, such as high cholesterol.

- Some consumers may find they cannot afford to buy functional foods on a regular basis, as these tend to cost more to buy than non-fortified versions of the same food.

- Functional foods only provide the health benefits while they are consumed, so if the consumer stops buying/eating them, the health benefits are lost.

- Probiotic drinks may have been proven to improve digestive health, but consumers need to be aware of the fact that such drinks can be high in sugar to make them more palatable.

GENETICALLY MODIFIED (GM) FOODS

Genetic modification involves taking genes from cells from one plant or animal and introducing them into the cell of another plant or animal in order to produce a desired characteristic. An example of this is taking the anti-freeze gene found in Arctic fish and introducing it into strawberries so that the strawberry plants aren't affected by frost.

No GM crops are currently being grown commercially in the UK, but imported GM commodities, especially soya, are being used mainly for animal feed. Most current GM crops are insect-resistant or herbicide-tolerant, to make pest and weed control easier for farmers. The main crop species in which these GM traits have been introduced are soya, maize, cotton and oilseed rape. The Food Standards Agency leads on the safety of GM food.

VIDEO LINK

Head to the BrightRED Digital Zone and watch the GM Foods clip to find out about the steps involved in the genetic modification of organisms.

Key points:

- Genetically modified crops, such as maize or tomatoes, will be more efficient for farmers to grow and will use fewer pesticides, which is good for consumers who want to be environmentally friendly.

- Some consumers from certain religions may not be happy with the fact that animal genes could have been used to modify some plants.

- Consumers may not want to buy or consume GM foods if they are uncertain about the long-term health implications of the process.

contd

- It is possible for genetic modification to reduce or remove allergy-causing properties in some foods, e.g. removing lactose from milk so that lactose-intolerant people can consume dairy produce.

- GM can offer consumers foods with enhanced nutritional value, e.g. genetically modifying plants with a fish gene so that the plant provides a source of omega 3.

HYDROPONICS

Hydroponics involves growing plants in a substance other than soil – usually a solution of water that contains all the nutrients the plant needs for growth.

Key points:

- Plants can be grown hydroponically anywhere, even when soil conditions are poor, meaning that consumers can always have access to freshly grown food regardless of where they live.

- Growing plants hydroponically gives control over the growth of the plant and what is added to the water, so highly nutritious plants can be produced.

- Due to the controlled environments in which the plants are grown, there is more consistency with the end results, plus a higher yield, meaning that consumers can be assured of a high-quality product.

- The equipment required to grow plants hydroponically is expensive, and this cost could be passed onto the consumer.

ONLINE TEST

Test yourself on functional and GM foods at www. brightredbooks.net/N5HFT

THINGS TO DO AND THINK ABOUT

1 The 20 types of food and drink listed here have been identified by Gary Williamson, professor of 'functional foods' at Leeds University, and he recommends that we should all make them part of our diets, as they offer antioxidants that help protect our bodies from damage by free radicals.

Your task is to develop a super-healthy product using at least 2 of the ingredients from the table. Design a recipe sheet to go along with it which explains the health benefits of your food product.

MENU FOR A RIPE OLD AGE

Apples: Provide polyphenols

Blackberries: High levels of anthocyanins

Black tea: Theaflavins

Blueberries: High levels of anthocyanins

Broccoli: A range of health-giving polyphenols

Cereal bran: High in fibre and phenolic acids

Cherries: Contain antioxidant anthocyanins

Cherry tomatoes: High levels of quercatin

Coffee: Phenolic acids

Cranberries: Procyanadin, which can prevent infections

Dark chocolate: Cocoa contains epicatechin

Green tea: Polyphenols

Oranges: Contain hesperedin, which aids a healthy heart

Peaches: Contain epicatechin and phenolic acids

Plums: Similar role to peaches

Raspberries: Contain anthocyanins

Red grapes: Anthocyanins and phenolic acids

Red onions: High levels of cancer-fighting quercatin

Spinach: Polyphenols

Strawberries: Contain anthocyanins and ellagic acid

2 Watch this clip: http://www.bbc.co.uk/learningzone/clips/an-application-of-genetic-modification-in-food/7133.html. It explores a practical application of genetic modification. Investigate the issues raised by this clip, including genetic modification, omega 3 fatty acids and sustainability. Produce a poster/leaflet/presentation that highlights your findings, where you address the key question posed – would you eat the omega 3 plant?

3 Research and debate the similarities and differences between *genetic modification*, *cloning* and *selective breeding*. Consider any ethical issues that surround them.

TECHNOLOGICAL DEVELOPMENTS AFFECTING CONSUMERS' CHOICE OF FOOD 4

The next technological advances we will explore are irradiation, modified-atmosphere packaging (MAP) and nanotechnology.

This picture shows the Radura, which is the international symbol indicating that a food product has been irradiated.

DON'T FORGET

Delaying the ripening of fruits and vegetables could be seen as an advantage or a disadvantage!

IRRADIATION

This is the process of preventing food spoilage by exposing food to ionising energy (or radiation) to extend its shelf life. It is similar to X-raying the food. The process does not make the food radioactive. In the UK at present, only herbs and spices are irradiated – and, by law, all irradiated food must be described as such on the label.

Key points:

- There is some nutritional loss when food is irradiated, especially vitamins B and C, which means that consumers may not be getting the nutritional content they expect from certain foods.

- The delay in ripening might mean that consumers think they are choosing fresh fruit and vegetables, when in fact they are getting older products that have been irradiated to allow them to last longer.

- Many consumers link irradiation with nuclear technology and would not want to purchase foods that had been irradiated, as they have concerns about how it affects their long-term health.

- Irradiation reduces food spoilage by micro-organisms, reducing the risk of food poisoning and making the food safer to eat for consumers.

- Irradiation delays the ripening of fruit and the sprouting of vegetables, which may be good as it allows consumers to get fruit and vegetables which are in peak condition, thereby expanding consumers' choices.

- Irradiation can completely sterilise food, which makes it fit to eat for those patients in hospital who have a weakened immune system.

MODIFIED-ATMOSPHERE PACKAGING (MAP)

This is a way of extending the shelf life of fresh food products without the use of artificial preservatives. Fresh food doesn't last forever; it spoils. MAP aims to seal fresh food in a package containing a mixture of gases which slows down oxidation and bacterial growth. Oxygen is reduced, and CO_2 and nitrogen are increased. MAP is used to package foods such as: cold meats, cheese, salad leaves, fresh pasta.

VIDEO LINK

Have a look at the clip to see how MAP works: www.brightredbooks.net/N5HFT

contd.

Key points:

- Consumers benefit from fresh foods lasting for longer due to the shelf life being extended without the use of additives.

- The food products look attractive as there is no oxidation due to the change in gases within the packaging, which may encourage consumers to buy.

- Consumers know that they are getting good-quality food, as MAP can only extend the shelf life of food in a peak condition when packaged; but this may mean they have to pay a little more for the product.

- The fact that the food is packaged may be a concern to some consumers who like to be environmentally friendly.

NANOTECHNOLOGY

Nanotechnology is a science that manipulates materials by controlling their shape and size. These particles are extremely small (a nanometre is one thousand-millionth of a metre). Nano-sized particles occur naturally in food; however, new technology is developing the ability to engineer nanomaterials. Currently only a few products containing engineered nanomaterials are available worldwide: for example, in Australia, a brand of bread contains nano-capsules of fish oil to provide omega 3 fatty acids. The food industry is researching: (1) how to use this technology to produce foods with the same taste but lower in fat/salt/sugar, (2) encapsulation of flavours, and (3) the development of food packaging that could change colour so as to 'tell' the consumer when it was no longer fit to eat.

Key points:

- There is still limited scientific data regarding how safe nano-technology is to the human body, therefore some consumers would avoid such products on health grounds.

- Companies are developing nano-materials that could be used for food packaging to reduce food spoilage, thus increasing the shelf life of products for consumers.

- Nano-sensors are being developed that can detect bacteria, such as salmonella, at a food-processing plant, thus reducing the chance of consumers getting food poisoning from infected food.

- At the moment, the development of nano-technology in food production may be too expensive to implement on a commercial scale, therefore any products that do become available may be expensive for consumers to buy.

ONLINE TEST

Test yourself on irradiation, MAP and nanotechnology at www.brightredbooks.net/N5HFT

THINGS TO DO AND THINK ABOUT

Imagine you work for a food-packaging company which has developed the nanotechnology within its packaging so that it changes colour when food is no longer fit to eat. Develop a poster, or a different piece of marketing, to advertise your product.

TECHNOLOGICAL DEVELOPMENTS AFFECTING CONSUMERS' CHOICE OF FOOD 5

The last of the developments which we will explore here are smart ingredients, ultra-heat treating (UHT) and vacuum packing.

SMART INGREDIENTS

These are natural products that have been changed in some way to make them behave in a different, more useful, way. Some examples of smart ingredients include:

Fat-replacers

These are used by food manufacturers, mostly in the production of low-fat products.

- Their chemical make-up means they are too large to be absorbed by the body, so can help as part of a low-calorie diet; however, some, like Olestra, can cause anal leakage.

- They are also free from cholesterol, so can help reduce the risk of coronary heart disease for consumers.

Bulk and intense sweeteners

Intense sweeteners, such as aspartame, which is made from amino acids, are 180 times sweeter than sugar and are used in soft drinks.

Bulk sweeteners, such as Xylitol, made from the bark of the birch tree, are of similar sweetness to sugar but with 33% fewer calories. Xylitol is used in sugar-free confectionery, where it is less harmful to teeth.

- Artificial sweeteners can be used in the 'lite' food market, so providing consumers with a product that can help as part of a weight-reduction diet.

- Some artificial sweeteners do not need insulin to be metabolised and are therefore suitable to be eaten by diabetics, increasing their choice of foods.

- Some consumers are concerned about possible health effects of artificial sweeteners, so would avoid eating products containing them.

- Some artificial sweeteners cause a laxative effect if consumed in excess, which limits the amount consumers can eat of certain products.

Modified starches

There are over 300 modified starches available for manufacturers to use in a wide range of food products. These can be grouped into pre-gelatinised starches and chemically modified starches. Pre-gelatinised starches are used in products such as cup-a-soups and pot noodles. Chemically modified starches have the ability to thicken without being heated and remain stable during processing.

- Pre-gelatinised starch allows food products to be thickened without the application of heat, which saves busy consumers preparation time.

- Modified starch absorbs more water, and, when added to products to be frozen, prevents them from falling apart when defrosted.

- Modified starches have similar mouthfeel properties to fat, meaning a small amount could be used instead of fat in a sauce, giving the consumer a lower-fat product.

ULTRA-HIGH TEMPERATURE/ULTRA-HEAT-TREATED (UHT)

This is a sterilising process where foods are heated to around 140°C for a few seconds to kill any bacteria present. The product is then rapidly cooled and sealed in an airtight container. It is a process mostly used on milk and fruit juices, allowing them to keep for months at room temperature.

- Increased shelf life, at room temperature, allows consumers to keep UHT products for long periods of time, reducing the need for shopping trips

- The UHT process ensures that all bacteria are killed off, thus providing a safe product for consumers

- Can be bought in bulk and easily stored in a cupboard, therefore useful for consumers who live in remote areas or for emergencies during bad weather

- Some consumers do not like the smell or taste of UHT milk, which is a result of the heat-treatment process, so they would avoid buying it.

VACUUM PACKING

Products are placed into an airtight pack, the air is sucked out, and the package is sealed. The lack of oxygen reduces the growth of aerobic bacteria and prevents spoilage by oxidation. Vacuum packing is used for foods such as bacon and cheese.

- Vacuum packing extends the shelf life of any perishable food product by up to 3 times its refrigerated life

- Suitable products that have been bought in bulk can be frozen and will not suffer from freezer burn due to the strong packaging

- Once the package is opened, it needs to be stored in a fridge and re-covered to prevent it drying out.

THINGS TO DO AND THINK ABOUT

1 Why not make up a tarsia involving some of the terminology from technological developments and their meanings? Use it as a revision tool with your classmates.

2 Select one of the technological developments explored in this chapter. Think about some food products or ingredients that link to your choice. Use these to make a food product. Justify your choice of dish.

VIDEO LINK

Have a look at the advert from Tetra Pak which shows their UHT process: www.brightredbooks.net/N5HFT

DON'T FORGET

Aerobic bacteria need oxygen present in order to grow and multiply, whereas **anaerobic** bacteria can grow without oxygen being present.

ONLINE TEST

Test yourself on smart ingredients, UHT and vacuum packing at www.brightredbooks.net/N5HFT

HOW ORGANISATIONS PROTECT CONSUMERS' INTERESTS 1

When you buy goods or services, the law gives you consumer rights. These protect you from being treated unfairly.

In this unit, you will be required to identify at least **two organisations** that protect the interests of consumers. You will also need to include a **description of one main role of each organisation** in respect of consumers' interests.

Organisations include:

- Advertising Standards Authority
- Consumers' Association/Which?
- Citizens Advice Scotland
- Environmental Health Department
- Scottish Food Standards Agency
- Trading Standards

For now, let's look at the first three organisations on the list: Advertising Standards Authority, Consumers' Association/Which? and Citizens Advice Scotland.

DON'T FORGET

Head to the BrightRED Digital Zone and find links to all the organisations which protect the interests of consumers.

ADVERTISING STANDARDS AUTHORITY (ASA)

Since 1961, the ASA's aim has been to protect consumers and to promote responsible advertising. Its job is to regulate UK advertisements to ensure that they are truthful and socially responsible.

- The ASA makes sure that all advertisers in the UK follow the Advertising Codes, which ensures that ads targeted at children do not contain any content that will cause them harm.

- The ASA assesses, against an EU Register of approved health claims, adverts for food and drink products that make health claims. If these don't appear in the Register, the ads will not be approved, thus protecting consumers from misleading claims.

- No advertisements for foods that are high in fat/salt/sugar are allowed to appear on dedicated children's TV channels.

- The ASA acts upon consumer complaints made regarding advertisements that members of the public feel are misleading or offensive.

DON'T FORGET

As part of your course assignment, you will be asked to provide information about your food product in relation to a range of topic areas, one of which is advertising/marketing, so you may wish to take account of what you have learned about the ASA.

CASE STUDY: VITAMINWATER

Coca-Cola Great Britain (Vitaminwater) – April 2011

The ASA considered that consumers would not expect a drink advertised as 'nutritious' to have the equivalent of four or five teaspoons of added sugar. Because Vitaminwater contained about a quarter of a consumer's recommended daily intake of sugar, the description of Vitaminwater as 'nutritious' was considered to be misleading, so the ad was banned.

CONSUMERS' ASSOCIATION/WHICH?

The Consumers' Association trades under the name 'Which?'. It is a not-for-profit organisation. Members pay to subscribe to a monthly magazine and a range of services. The money that members pay is used to fund testing of products and to pay for campaigns that support consumers' rights. You will not be able to get help with an individual complaint from the Consumers' Association unless you subscribe/join as a member.

- Which? campaigns to get a fairer deal for all consumers.

- Which? undertakes research and publishes expert, unbiased reports that consumers can use to make informed choices when buying goods and services.

- Which? Local gives consumers the option of recommending local traders in their own area.

- Which? awards BEST BUY ratings to products if they perform consistently well in laboratory tests, and has DON'T BUY ratings for products that have performed extremely poorly in Which? tests.

 ONLINE

Have a look at the Which? food and health campaigns: www.brightredbooks.net/ N5HFT. Why not log onto the Which? website and have your say?

CITIZENS ADVICE BUREAUX (CAB)/CITIZENS ADVICE SCOTLAND (CAS)

Citizens Advice Scotland (CAS) is a national umbrella body that provides essential services to Scottish Citizens Advice Bureaux. Citizens Advice Bureaux are independent, local charities that are members of Citizens Advice Scotland. Bureaux provide advice and information to people in need in over 250 locations. The aims of the Scottish CAB Service are to ensure that individuals do not suffer through lack of knowledge of their rights and responsibilities, or of the services available to them, or through an inability to express their need effectively.

- Provides free, independent and confidential advice on a wide range of consumer issues, including debt, health, housing and consumer issues.

- Aims to answer questions about benefit entitlements, support benefit applications and help with appeals against unfair decisions.

- Provides debt and money advice and can work with people in debt to put a repayment plan in place.

- Helps with work-related problems, e.g. questions about terms and conditions or support with redundancy/dismissal.

- Provides support with consumer issues, e.g. help to deal with problems with internet service providers or how to complain about faulty goods.

 VIDEO LINK

Visit www.brightredbooks. net/N5HFT and watch the CAB clip to get an insight into the work of the Citizens Advice Bureau.

 ONLINE TEST

Check how well you've learned about the Advertising Standards Authority, Consumers' Association/Which? and Citizens Advice Scotland at www.brightredbooks.net/ N5HFT

THINGS TO DO AND THINK ABOUT

Your teacher needs to buy some new food processors to use in school. She has asked you to come up with a suggestion as to which model you think she should buy. You must justify your choice. Use the Which? website to help you with your research (www.which.co.uk).

HOW ORGANISATIONS PROTECT CONSUMERS' INTERESTS 2

Now that you've learned about the Advertising Standards Authority, Consumers' Association/ Which? and Citizens Advice Scotland, let's have a look at the Environmental Health Department, Scottish Food Standards Agency and Trading Standards.

ENVIRONMENTAL HEALTH DEPARTMENT

Environmental health is the responsibility of local authorities. In Scotland, there are seven key areas that environmental health deals with: Food Safety, Food Standards, Occupational Health and Safety, Public Health, Waste Management, Built Environment, and Pollution Control.

Environmental Health (or Enforcement) Officers are involved with inspection, education that provides advice and guidance to businesses and consumers, and enforcement of consumer legislation, specifically laws relating to food hygiene and safety.

- EHOs undertake a programme of inspections, where they go into local food businesses to check that they are following the standards laid down by the Food Safety Act 1990.

- EHOs investigate complaints about food, including complaints about the hygiene of premises.

- They follow a programme of regularly sampling food, in particular locally produced food, to check that it is safe for consumption.

- EHOs investigate reported cases of food poisoning.

- EHOs can seize unsafe or dangerous goods.

- EHOs can serve improvement notices to food premises that are not complying with food hygiene regulations. In extreme cases, they can request that premises be closed immediately if there is a threat to public health.

VIDEO LINK

Watch the clip from the BBC programme *The Food Inspectors* to see how EHOs go about a kitchen inspection: www. brightredbooks.net/N5HFT

ONLINE

Check out the Scottish Food Standards Agency website to find out more.

ONLINE

Follow the link at www. brightredbooks.net/N5HFT to find out more about the Food Hygiene Information Scheme in Scotland.

ONLINE

Visit the Digital Zone and use the link to check out the ratings for food businesses in your local area.

SCOTTISH FOOD STANDARDS AGENCY

Their job is to improve food safety and standards in Scotland and protect the health of Scotland's population in relation to food. Food safety and standards are devolved matters, and legislation governing Scotland is determined by the Scottish Parliament.

- The FSA provides information and advice to consumers to help them make healthier food choices.

- The FSA undertakes sampling and testing of food products to check that the contents match what it says on the label, e.g. to make sure a product advertised as a beefburger doesn't contain horse meat!

- The FSA issues withdrawal or recall notices if allergy labelling is incorrect and there is a risk of a consumer eating a product they may be allergic to.

- The FSA assesses and reviews food additives to ensure that they are safe to be in foods, and will take legal action where problems are found.

contd

- The FSA, in partnership with local authorities, is responsible for administering the Food Hygiene Information Scheme, which helps consumers to choose where to eat out or shop for food by giving them information about the hygiene standards in restaurants, cafés, takeaways, hotels and food shops.

European food safety legislation requires that all food businesses, including caterers, apply food safety management procedures based on the principles of **Hazard Analysis and Critical Control Point** (HACCP) to their business.

CookSafe was introduced to help catering businesses in Scotland to understand and implement a HACCP-based food safety system.

ONLINE

Check out the website for more on CookSafe: www.brightredbooks.net/N5HFT

TRADING STANDARDS

Trading Standards in Scotland are part of local authorities, and they aim to ensure fair trading to protect consumers and businesses from unfair and unsafe trading practices. They also enforce consumer protection laws. For example, you have up to 5 years after purchase to take civil action if a problem has been discovered; and Trading Standards officers can support you in making a claim in the small-claims court, up to a limit of £3000.

- Age-related sales – Trading Standards Officers undertake random checks to make sure that shops are not selling cigarettes/alcohol/DVDs/fireworks to minors (anyone under age).

- Weights and measures – Trading Standards enforce the Weights and Measures Act 1985 by checking to make sure that bars and pubs do not serve short measures of alcohol, or that a supermarket deli counter's weighing scales are accurate, so that customers get the exact amount they are paying for.

- Product counterfeiting – Trading Standards regularly visit markets to check that goods being sold are not fake. They have the power to seize the goods and take legal action against the trader selling the counterfeit goods.

- Trading Standards protect consumers by making sure that a trader does not falsely describe goods they are selling. For example, if a market trader has a sign saying 'organic potatoes for sale', they have to prove that these have indeed been produced organically.

DON'T FORGET

You need to know what your rights are in order to protect them. The Office of Fair Trading has a range of short advice films about your consumer rights (http://www.youtube.com/OFTWebEditor). Why not have a look?

ONLINE TEST

Check how well you've learned about all of the organisations mentioned in this topic online at www.brightredbooks.net/N5HFT

THINGS TO DO AND THINK ABOUT

Watch this BBC clip from *The Food Inspectors* programme on the dangers of cooked rice: http://www.bbc.co.uk/programmes/p014503p. Undertake some additional research into the bacterium *Bacillus cereus*. Design a poster that highlights the dangers of cooked rice and the action steps that should be taken to prevent the risk of food poisoning. Make a rice-based dish, and produce a label which includes clear storage instructions.

FOOD LABELLING 1

Assessment for this topic requires you to **identify at least four pieces of information** from a food label. You must then **explain how four pieces of information** on food labels can help consumers to make informed choices. In addition, in section 2 of the HFT Assignment, you will be asked to provide information about your food product in two areas, including: labelling, packaging and nutritional analysis.

LABELLING POLICY

The Food Standards Agency in Scotland is responsible for policy on food labelling, including nutritional labelling. However, there are also European Union rules that need to be followed. For example, from 2014, new food-labelling rules will require country of origin for meat to be stated; and there will be a minimum font size for labels to ensure that customers can read the label and see clearly what is in their food. The Food Standards Agency Scotland also carries out checks to make sure that product contents match what is stated on the label – for example, if it says beef, it should not contain any horse meat.

The law states that some information <u>must</u> be included on all food packaging (statutory).

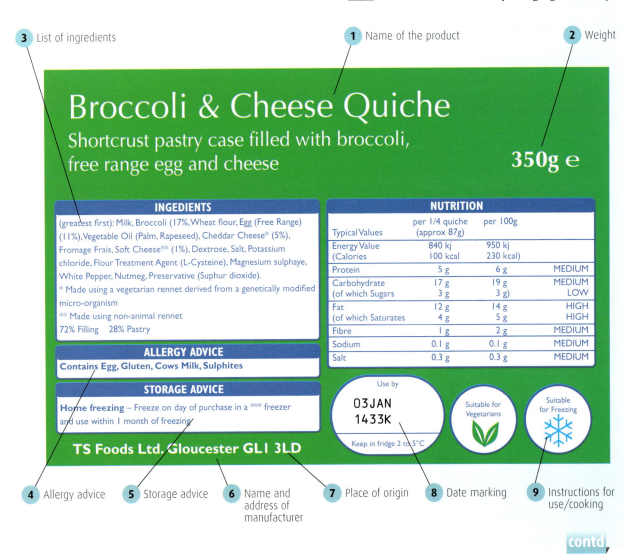

3 List of ingredients   **1** Name of the product   **2** Weight

Broccoli & Cheese Quiche
Shortcrust pastry case filled with broccoli, free range egg and cheese

350g e

INGEDIENTS
(greatest first): Milk, Broccoli (17%, Wheat flour, Egg (Free Range) (11%), Vegetable Oil (Palm, Rapeseed), Cheddar Cheese* (5%), Fromage Frais, Soft Cheese** (1%), Dextrose, Salt, Potassium chloride, Flour Treatment Agent (L-Cysteine), Magnesium sulphaye, White Pepper, Nutmeg, Preservative (Suphur dioxide).
* Made using a vegetarian rennet derived from a genetically modified micro-organism
** Made using non-animal rennet
72% Filling   28% Pastry

ALLERGY ADVICE
Contains Egg, Gluten, Cows Milk, Sulphites

STORAGE ADVICE
Home freezing – Freeze on day of purchase in a *** freezer and use within 1 month of freezing

TS Foods Ltd. Gloucester GL1 3LD

NUTRITION

Typical Values	per 1/4 quiche (approx 87g)	per 100g	
Energy Value (Calories	840 kj 100 kcal	950 kj 230 kcal)	
Protein	5 g	6 g	MEDIUM
Carbohydrate (of which Sugars	17 g 3 g	19 g 3 g)	MEDIUM LOW
Fat (of which Saturates	12 g 4 g	14 g 5 g	HIGH HIGH
Fibre	1 g	2 g	MEDIUM
Sodium	0.1 g	0.1 g	MEDIUM
Salt	0.3 g	0.3 g	MEDIUM

Use by
03JAN 1433K
Keep in fridge 2 to 5°C

Suitable for Vegetarians

Suitable for Freezing

4 Allergy advice   **5** Storage advice   **6** Name and address of manufacturer   **7** Place of origin   **8** Date marking   **9** Instructions for use/cooking

contd

Statutory information on food label	How it helps consumers to make informed choices
(1) Name of the food product (or a description of what the product is)	• Consumers know exactly what the food is • Allows consumers to take account of likes and dislikes • Prevents consumers from being deceived, e.g. they will know that a product called strawberry jam must contain strawberries
(2) Weight or volume. Some products carry the 'e' mark. This is not compulsory. It means that the average quantity must be accurate but the exact weight of each pack may vary slightly.	• Allows consumers to work out how much of the product they will need for the number of people they have to feed • Helps the consumer to work out value for money • Allows consumers to compare like-for-like products
(3) List of ingredients, in descending order of weight	• Lets consumers see exactly what the product contains, so they can take account of likes and dislikes • Allows consumers see at a glance if any ingredients listed are ones they may have an allergy to • Allows a comparison with similar products, e.g. can check the percentage of meat in similar products
(4) Allergy advice – EU law requires food manufacturers to list 12 potentially allergic ingredients: gluten, eggs, fish, crustaceans, peanuts, soy, milk and dairy products, nuts, celery, mustard, sesame seeds and sulphites.	• Provides health protection for consumers, as they can avoid products that contain any ingredients they may be allergic to
(5) Storage advice	• Informs the consumer how the product must be stored in order to ensure that the food remains safe to eat
(6) Name and address of the manufacturer	• Allows the consumer to contact the manufacturer in case of a complaint • Lets consumers know where to return a product to in case there is a safety recall
(7) Place of origin	• Allows consumers to make an informed choice, as they may choose to avoid buying food from certain countries on moral grounds
(8) Date marking • **Best before** will be appropriate for the vast majority of foods and indicates the period for which a food can reasonably be expected to retain its optimal condition (e.g. it will not be stale) and so relates to the **quality** of the food. • **Use by** is the required form of date mark for those foods which are highly perishable from a microbiological point of view and which are likely after a relatively short period to present a risk of food poisoning, and so relates to the **safety** of the food.	• Consumers know that they must eat food before the 'use by' date in order to prevent any risk of food poisoning • 'Best before' date advises consumers about the quality of a product if they choose to eat it after the date marked • Date marking helps consumers with stock control when storing food at home • Following date marking can help consumers to avoid food waste
(9) Instructions for use/cooking	• By looking at the label, consumers will know if they have the time/equipment/skills to prepare or cook the product • Ensures that consumers cook or use the product correctly/prevents any risks to health

ONLINE

Check out the page on the BrightRED Digital Zone for an overview of the new food-labelling regulations.

DON'T FORGET

Statutory = must be included by law. Mandatory = up to manufacturers to decide if they want to include it on their product's labels or not, but if they do, they cannot make false claims.

ONLINE TEST

Check how well you've learned about food labelling at www.brightredbooks.net/N5HFT

THINGS TO DO AND THINK ABOUT

Design and make a batch of shortbread by putting your own slant on a classic shortbread recipe. Design a label for your new shortbread product.

Your label should be clear to read and understand, and should include all the information legally required for a food product.

Design a checklist that you can use to self-evaluate your label to make sure it contains all of the statutory information that must be there by law.

FOOD LABELLING 2

VOLUNTARY LABELLING

The following items are not legally required to be on a food label, but are nevertheless good practice and are often voluntarily included on packaging:

Voluntary information on food label	How it helps consumers to make informed choices
• Illustration of product	• Lets consumers see what the product looks like before buying it • May give ideas within the picture for how to serve the product • Having a picture will help consumers to see what a product looks like if they are unfamiliar with the name or don't know what the product is
• Price	• Allows consumers to know straight away if they can afford the product • Lets consumers make decisions about value for money • Consumers can compare prices between similar products before deciding which to buy
• Nutritional information	• Helps consumers who are following a low-calorie/fat/salt/sugar diet • Informs consumers who need to control their food intake for health reasons • Allows consumers to add up calories if calorie-counting as part of a diet • Helps consumers to choose between products • Can help consumers to choose products that will help them to follow a healthy diet
• Bar code	• Can speed up the sale process, especially if the consumer uses a self-scan system • Should reduce the chances of consumers being wrongly charged for a product • As it allows stores to control stock, it should mean there is more chance a store will have products in stock that a consumer is looking for
• Recycling information	• May influence a consumer's choice of product if they are concerned about the environment • May help to save consumers time when sorting out their recycling for collection • On-pack guidance will help consumers' understanding regarding whether or not a product's packaging can be recycled
• Customer information labels, e.g. vegetarian seedling symbol or organic logo	• Provides assurances for consumers that the product has met the requirements laid down by the body awarding the symbol
• Freezer star rating	• Provides consumers with advice about the best way to store/care for the food • Consumers will know how long they can store the food for

DON'T FORGET

There are guidelines to tell you if a food is high or low in fat, saturated fat, salt or sugar. These are:
Total fat
High: more than 20g of fat per 100g
Low: 3g of fat or less per 100g
Saturated fat
High: more than 5g of saturated fat per 100g
Low: 1.5g of saturated fat or less per 100g
Sugars
High: more than 15g of total sugars per 100g
Low: 5g of total sugars or less per 100g
Salt
High: more than 1.5g of salt per 100g (or 0.6g sodium)
Low: 0.3g of salt or less per 100g (or 0.1g sodium)

FRONT-OF-PACK FOOD LABELLING

The UK has a voluntary system of front-of-pack food labelling. A combination of guideline daily amounts, colour coding and 'high, medium or low' wording is used to show how much fat, salt and sugar and how many calories are in each product. This is a mixture of 'traffic light labelling' and 'Guideline Daily Amounts'.

Guideline Daily Amounts

Guideline Daily Amounts (GDAs) are guidelines about the approximate amount of particular nutrients and calories required for a healthy diet. Because individual requirements for calories and nutrients are different for all people, GDAs are not intended as targets. Instead, they are intended to give a useful indication of how a particular nutrient or amount of calories fits into a daily diet.

Guideline daily amounts (GDA)			
Source: Institute of Grocery Distribution			
	Women	Men	Children (5–10 years)
Calories (kcal)	2000	2500	1800
Protein	45g	55g	24g
Carbohydrate	230g	300g	220g
Fat	70g	95g	70g
Fibre	24g	24g	15g
Sodium	2.4g	2.4g	1.4g

EXEMPLIFICATION OF ASSESSMENT

In this example, for Assessment Standard 1.5, the learner has chosen **four** of the pieces of information from a standard food label and has given a description as to how each of these four pieces of information helps the consumer make informed choices.

ONLINE

Follow the link from the Digital Zone to launch a sample label.

Explanations

1) **Traffic Lighting** – lets the consumer see that this product is high in saturated fat, as it has a red warning, so someone watching their weight or cutting their fat intake knows to avoid it.

2) **Ingredients list** – lets the consumer see exactly what ingredients the product contains, with the largest amount being first on the list.

3) **Allergens** – allows the consumer to avoid the product if an ingredient is listed that they are allergic to – in this case, someone with coeliac disease may avoid it, as it contains gluten.

4) **Date marking** – in this case, 'best before' informs the consumer when they should eat the product before. Eating after that date may mean that the quality is not as good.

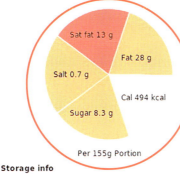

Plum Oaty Cereal Bars *(2 portions)*

Sat fat 13 g
Fat 28 g
Salt 0.7 g
Cal 494 kcal
Sugar 8.3 g
Per 155g Portion

Storage info
Store in an airtight container.

Allergens
gluten, oats, wheat, wheat gluten

Use By
Best before 08/2015

Manufactured By
Plum Products Health & Food Tech Products Test Kitchen TK8 1PT

Net weight 310g

Ingredients
plums (32%), flour (24%), margarine (19%), rolled oats (16%), cereal (8%)

	Per 100g	Per portion (155g)	GDA
			%GDA*
Energy kJ	1332 kJ	2065 kJ	25%
Energy kcal	319 kcal	494 kcal	25%
Protein	5.6 g	8.7 g	19%
Carbohydrate	34 g	52 g	23%
of which sugar	5.4 g	8.3 g	9%
Total Fat	18 g	28 g	40%
of which saturates**	8.1 g	13 g	63%
Fibre	5.1 g	7.9 g	33%
Salt	0.5 g	0.7 g	12%

* Percentage Daily Values are based on a 2,000 calorie diet for an average adult.
Your Daily Values may be higher or lower depending on your calorie needs.
** Data for some ingredients is not available

ONLINE TEST

Check how well you've learned about Food Labelling at www.brightredbooks.net/N5HFT

THINGS TO DO AND THINK ABOUT

1   Look at this food label (or a food label of your choice). Identify four pieces of information from the label. Explain how four pieces of information from the label help consumers to make informed choices. (NB: you may choose to explain the same four pieces or choose different pieces.)

2   Design a questionnaire that will allow you to find out about pupils' or the public's awareness of the information found on food labels. You may want to include some common symbols or ask about Guideline Daily Amounts to check for understanding.

PACKAGING

THE HISTORY OF PACKAGING

Timeline:

Prehistoric:
Leaves and skin hides used for wrapping

Early civilisation:
Pottery is first made in Japan (10 000 BC)

Pre-1800:
Grocers measure out and wrap food in paper

1800–1850:
The first airtight glass container is created (1809)

1850–1900:
Glass bottles with screw stoppers are manufactured (1870s)

1900–1940s:
Waxed paper cartons are used (1910s) Polythene is invented in Britain (1933) Plastic is used as a packaging material (1940s)

1950s–present:
Aseptic milk carton invented by Tetra Pak (1950s) PET bottle for carbonated drinks developed (1970s) 100% biodegradable 'potatopak' packaging developed (2005)

THE ENVIRONMENTAL IMPACT OF MODERN PACKAGING

In 2010, the UK disposed of an estimated 10.8 million tonnes of packaging waste, of which around 67% was recovered. This is a significant achievement: in 1998, only 27% of packaging waste was recovered; however, the government is keen to continue to reduce the amount of packaging going into landfill year on year.

Therefore, for environmental reasons, there is a push for products to be sold with less packaging; however, food does need some form of packaging. Packaging protects food from damage, can increase the shelf life of food, provides information and makes food products easier to handle, transport and store. The choice of packaging depends very much upon the food it will contain.

Different materials can be used for packaging:

contd

PACKAGING MATERIAL	ADVANTAGES	DISADVANTAGES	USES	RECYCLING SYMBOLS
Plastic	• versatile • resistant to acids/chemicals • lightweight • easy to print on • cheap to produce • water-resistant • heat-resistant	• thermoplastics are not sustainable, as they are made from non-renewable resources • if not recycled, they take up a lot of landfill space	• milk cartons • juice bottles • sauces • bags	♲1 PETE ♲2 HDPE ♲3 V ♲4 LDPE ♲5 PP ♲6 PS ♲7 OTHER
Glass	• reusable • heat-resistant • recyclable • keeps shape • low cost	• fragile/breakable • safety issues • heavy	• jars of sauces • alcoholic drinks • pickles	
Metal	• recyclable • lightweight • strong • withstands heat processing	• may react with food • cannot be used in microwaves	• soup cans • takeaway containers • bottle tops	(alu)
Card/paper	• easy to print on • cheap to produce • biodegradable • recyclable • can be moulded • can be coated • lightweight	• not water-resistant • easily damaged	• fruit-juice cartons • egg boxes • tea bags	

Environmentally friendly packaging causes less damage to the environment. There are three types:

- **Reusable packaging** can be cleaned and reused. For example, glass milk bottles are reused.

- **Recyclable packaging** is made of materials that can be used again, usually after processing. Recyclable materials include glass, metal, card and paper.

- **Biodegradable packaging** will easily break down in the soil or the atmosphere, e.g. 'potatopak'.

THINGS TO DO AND THINK ABOUT

- As a practice assessment for unit outcome 2, select **reducing food waste** as your factor that affects consumer food choices. Use the website http://scotland. lovefoodhatewaste.com/ to come up with some food products which address this factor. Make your chosen food product. Finally, explain why your chosen food product helps to meet the factor – i.e. how does it help to reduce food waste?

- You might want to design suitable packaging for the product you have made. What material would you use, and why? Why not design a label for your product? Get a fellow classmate to peer-evaluate your package idea and label.

- Investigate the range of different types of packaging available in supermarkets for soup. Develop your own soup recipe. Design packaging and a label for your soup. Explain your choice of packaging. Undertake some sensory evaluation to find out how successful your soup is, and get views on your ideas for packaging/labelling.

ONLINE

Follow the Zero Waste link to find out more about Scotland's plans to reduce the amount of waste. Why not look at their Love Food Hate Waste campaign? It's packed with practical hints, tips and recipe ideas for reducing food waste. Use the information here to design a poster/leaflet/presentation.

DON'T FORGET

You can do your bit. **Reduce** the amount of the Earth's resources that you use. **Reuse**, don't just bin it; could someone else make use of it? **Recycle**: can the materials be made into something new?

ONLINE TEST

Check how well you've learned about food packaging at www.brightredbooks.net/N5HFT

COURSE ASSESSMENT

QUESTION PAPER

The National 5 Health and Food Technology course has two components that make up the final assessment: (1) Question paper worth 50 marks; (2) Assignment worth 50 marks.

THE QUESTION PAPER: AN OVERVIEW

The question paper will assess your ability to apply the knowledge and understanding you have gained from studying the three units, via answering five exam questions.

There will be five questions in the paper, each question worth 10 marks. You will get 1 hour and 30 minutes to complete the paper and the questions in the paper will sample across the whole course.

DIETARY REFERENCE VALUE QUESTIONS

You will always find a Dietary Reference Value (DRV)-type question, which will involve you having to use your skills in 'evaluating' when you answer.

EXAMPLE:

A 45-year-old self-employed builder works long hours. He is overweight, has been diagnosed with diabetes and has been advised by his doctor to improve his diet.

Dietary Reference Values for men aged 19–50 years					
Energy (MJ)	Protein (g)	Vitamin A (mg)	Iron (mg)	Sodium (g)	Fibre (g)
11.50	55.5	700	8.7	1.6	18

Dietary analysis of his typical day's meals					
Energy (MJ)	Protein (g)	Vitamin A (µg)	Iron (mg)	Sodium (g)	Fibre (g)
13.20	62.0	530	5.5	2.3	13

The first thing to do is to look at his intake compared to the DRV table, and note down if the intake is high or low. Use a highlighter to do this, or write 'high/low' on your exam paper. This will help you when it comes to writing your answers. For example:

Energy (MJ)	Protein (g)	Vitamin A (µg)	Iron (mg)	Sodium (g)	Fibre (g)
13.20	62.0	530	5.5	2.3	13
+ High	+ High	– Low	– Low	+ High	– Low

In order to answer this question, you are required to **evaluate** by commenting on the suitability of the nutritional content of the meal in relation to the individual in the scenario. Choose the nutrients that you know most about first; that way, you can be confident your answer is showing you applying your knowledge. For example:

- The 45-year-old builder's meals contain more energy than he needs, so any extra will be converted into fat if not burned off.
- His meals do not provide him with enough iron, so he may feel tired, especially as he's working long hours as a builder.
- His fibre intake is low, which may increase his risk of suffering from bowel disorders.

contd

What you are doing here is (1) using information from the tables, e.g. stating he has eaten too much or too little of a particular nutrient, and then (2) giving an explanation, or consequence, as to why this is important to the person, given their circumstances – e.g. he works long hours as a builder, so he needs iron to provide him with oxygen or else he may feel tired. It can be helpful if you can think about linking your consequence to a dietary disease.

MORE EVALUATION QUESTIONS

Another type of 'evaluation' question you may find in the exam paper looks like this:

> The 45-year-old builder who works long hours and has been diagnosed with diabetes is considering joining his local Healthy Body Club.

- ■ Weekly weigh-in, measure and body stat recording
- ■ 15-minute educational and motivational group talk
- ■ 30-minute fat-burning work-out
- ■ Online work-out routines
- ■ Meal planning and recipe ideas
- ■ Detox plan

Evaluate the suitability of this activity for him using the features listed alongside.

Examples of suitable answers to this type of question are:

- Weekly weigh-in is a good idea for the builder, as it will give him an incentive to lose weight – **or**

- Weekly weigh-in is not such a good idea for the builder, as he works long hours so may struggle to make it to the weekly weigh-in and will lose motivation to attend

- 30-minute fat-burning work-out may be difficult for the builder to complete each week, as he works long hours and may be too tired to put in the effort needed to work out

- 15-minute educational talk will be good for the 45-year-old, as it could give him advice as to which foods to eat to help him control his diabetes.

What you are doing here to answer this type of question is (1) stating whether the bullet point of info is suitable or not, or is good or bad for the person mentioned in the scenario, then (2) explaining why it is either suitable or unsuitable, remembering to link your answer to the person mentioned in the scenario.

'IDENTIFY' AND 'GIVE REASONS FOR YOUR CHOICE'

The written exam paper will also contain question(s) where you are asked to **identify** and then **give reasons for your choice**. The first thing you will need to do is to identify the most suitable item from options in a table to meet the needs of the scenario you have been given. For an example of this style of question, turn to page 93.

ASSIGNMENT

THE ASSIGNMENT: AN OVERVIEW

The course assignment requires you to use the skills you have learned throughout the course to investigate a food or consumer issue. Through using a problem-solving approach, you will develop a suitable food product to meet the needs of the issue.

The assignment has four sections:
- (1) Planning — 20 marks
- (2) The product — 12 marks
- (3) Product testing — 10 marks
- (4) Reflection — 8 marks.

SQA will announce the food or consumer issue that you will be required to investigate. Examples of possible issues that you might have to investigate would be:

> Your local health board has reported an increase in the number of young people attending their diabetic clinic. The dietician who runs the clinic has asked you to develop a breakfast bar that would be suitable for diabetics.

> A local supermarket is planning a testing session to encourage customers to try their range of Fairtrade products. You have been asked to develop a dessert that incorporates Fairtrade ingredient(s).

SECTION 1: PLANNING

The first thing you are going to have to do is to identify the key issues from the scenario, followed by explaining the significance of the key issues to the scenario. For example, using the first issue above, you might identify the key issues as: 1. Diabetes and 2. Breakfast bar.

contd

For your explanations, you might note:

1. As there has been an increase in the number of young people with diabetes, I will need to find out more about the dietary needs of people suffering from diabetes so that I can take this into account when developing my product.

2. I have been asked to develop a breakfast bar, so it needs to: (1) be liked by those who will be eating it, (2) be suitable to eat on the go, and (3) provide energy to start the day.

The next stage is to undertake some **research** to obtain more information relating to the key points you have highlighted.

Key Issue 1.	Diabetes
What do I want to find out? i.e. the aim of my investigation is ... to find out nutritional factors that need to be taken into consideration for someone with diabetes.	
How am I going to do this? i.e. my method of investigation is ... I am going to search for information using the internet.	
Source of information: www.diabetes.co.uk or www.diabetes.org.uk What I found out: people suffering from diabetes should limit their intake of sugar and increase the amount of fruit and vegetables they eat. Some artificial sweeteners do not affect blood glucose levels so could be included in a diabetic's diet, but not too much as they can have a laxative effect if too many are eaten.	

Key Issue 2.	Breakfast bars
What do I want to find out? i.e. the aim of my investigation is ... to find out young people's likes and dislikes when it comes to breakfast bars.	
How am I going to do this? i.e. my method of investigation is ... a questionnaire to 20 young people.	
Source of information: www.surveymonkey.com	
What I found out: 18/20 wanted breakfast bars to contain oats. The preferred fruits were apple 15/20 and raspberry 16/20, and least liked was raisins. One person who completed my questionnaire had a nut allergy so would not eat a bar containing nuts.	

From this, you have to generate some ideas for a food product.

Now you have to decide which is the most appropriate product and give a detailed justification for your choice, before providing a detailed and accurate recipe for your new product.

DON'T FORGET

To get full marks here, two key issues must be identified correctly and the importance of these key issues fully explained.

DON'T FORGET

You have to use two underline research techniques and two underline sources. To help you here, refer to the 'Undertaking investigations' section earlier in the book, on pages 44–47.

DON'T FORGET

You need to provide at least three relevant ideas based on the results of research, all of which are accompanied by comments as to why they are or are not suitable.

DON'T FORGET

Your product can be based upon an existing recipe, but it must be adapted in some way to meet the aim of developing a new product.

SECTION 2: THE PRODUCT

In section 2, you must provide information about your product in <u>two</u> of the following areas:

- labelling
- advertising/marketing
- packaging
- costing
- nutritional analysis.

In order to achieve the 12 marks, you have to make sure that the information you provide is clear, accurate and relevant to the product. You must also provide justification for why this information is useful for the product and the scenario.

Labelling

Remember there are points of information that must be included on a label by law. Refresh your memory by looking through pages 80–83 earlier in the book.

Advertising/marketing

Don't forget what you learned about the work of the Advertising Standards Authority – see page 76 in the book. It's up to you how you want to display the information on how you might go about advertising or marketing your product. Some suggestions to consider include:

- Doing a storyboard that shows your ideas for an advert.
- Producing a script for a radio advert.
- Designing a magazine or newspaper advert.
- Creating a flyer that includes a money-off coupon.

Packaging

Refer back to pages 84–85 in the book to remind you of the different types of packaging available before you consider which type of packaging might be most appropriate for your product. Remember to take account of factors such as how it needs to be preserved, and how it would be transported and stacked on store shelves. You might decide to do a labelled drawing explaining your packaging ideas – or you could even make up the packaging and photograph it.

Costing

You will need to provide a breakdown cost of all ingredients. Don't forget to note down your source, e.g. supermarket website. Remember, working out a costing only shows the cost of the raw ingredients and will not take account of energy or labour or packaging costs. Also, a costing cannot be used to say that a product is good value for money or to infer that consumers will like it/buy it because of the cost.

Ingredient	Unit cost	Quantity	Cost	
			£	P
Plain flour	£0.30 per kg	100g		03
Butter	£0.98 for 250g	50g		20
Caster sugar	£1.05 per kg	50g		05
Total food cost				
Food cost per portion				

contd

ONLINE

You can get more information on labels by clicking the link to launch a sample label at www.brightredbooks.net/N5HFT

ONLINE

If your centre has a subscription to www.nutritionprogram.co.uk, you can input your recipe and click on the food label tab to produce your label.

VIDEO LINK

Watch the clip showing an advert for Kellogg's Cereal & Milk Bar to get some ideas: www.brightredbooks.net/N5HFT

DON'T FORGET

When undertaking a costing exercise, you need to round all figures up or down to the nearest penny.

Nutritional analysis

You will need to show the source of your data, e.g. relevant book, website or nutritional analysis programme. You may not need to provide analysis of every nutrient; think carefully about which nutrients are most relevant to the scenario, and include these.

> **EXAMPLE**
>
> The following nutritional analysis is from www.nutritionprogram.co.uk:
>
> **Recipe: Plum Oaty Cereal Bars**
>
> **ingredients:** plums (32%), flour (24%), margarine (19%), rolled oats (16%), cereal (8%)
>
> **net weight:** 310.0g **allergens:** gluten, oats, wheat, wheat gluten
>
> Nutrition Information
>
> | Nutrition | per 100g | per portion | women | men | child | traffic light |
> |---|---|---|---|---|---|---|
> | Energy | 1332 kJ | 2065 kJ | 25% | 20% | 27% | |
> | Energy | 319 kcal | 494 kcal | 25% | 20% | 27% | |
> | Protein | 5.6 g | 8.7 g | 19% | 16% | 36% | |
> | Carbohydrate | 34 g | 52 g | 23% | 17% | 24% | |
> | Fat | 18 g | 28 g | 40% | 29% | 40% | amber |

DON'T FORGET

Regardless as to which two areas you choose, you <u>must</u> make sure the information you provide is clear, accurate and relevant to the product. You must also provide justification for why this information is useful for the product and the scenario.

SECTION 3: PRODUCT TESTING

In section 3 of the assignment, you are required to undertake sensory testing of your product, followed by an analysis of the results obtained. 10 marks are available here if you:

1. Describe the test you plan to carry out and give reasons for why you have chosen this test

2. Carry out the sensory test and accurately record the results

3. Interpret the results and draw some conclusions as to what the testing told you about your product.

Before you start this section, read over pages 48–51 in the book to refresh your memory as to how to conduct a test session and to ensure that you have chosen the most appropriate test to give you the information you need.

It is a good idea to invite a minimum of 5 people to taste your product so that you can obtain enough data to provide valid results. Include a breakdown of <u>all</u> the results you obtain from the testing. A key is an essential way of making interpreting the data easy. Displaying your results in a table is a good idea.

Finally, you will need to provide at least **2** valid conclusions from the results of your testing. An example of this could be:

- 4 out of 5 tasters scored my product poor for texture. Comments tasters made highlighted that they were disappointed that the cereal bar was quite soggy and they would have preferred it to be crispier, so this is an area I will have to improve if I want my bar to be acceptable to the target group.

DON'T FORGET

You will need to provide detailed results presented accurately and in an appropriate manner if you want to gain all the marks available for this section of the assignment.

SECTION 4: REFLECTION

In this section, there are 8 marks available. You will be assessed on the relevance and depth of the points of evaluation you make in relation to the food product you have made.

To do this, you need to use the results of your research and sensory testing. You need to consider if there are any adaptations or improvements that you could make to your product in the light of your research. Finally, you must come up with a conclusion about how well the food product you made actually meets the needs of the initial scenario.

DON'T FORGET

You must make use of evidence shown in your assignment when making your comments/suggestions. Speculation is not acceptable.

EXTRA ACTIVITIES

MORE ACTIVITIES FOR 'THE BENEFITS TO HEALTH OF A BALANCED AND VARIED DIET' (pp 6-7)

1 If you have access to a nutritional analysis program, why not use the daily diet analysis section to check how balanced your own diet is? This can also be done via keeping, and analysing, your own food diary.

2 Undertake some research into an unusual vegetable or piece of fruit, e.g. okra, artichoke, celeriac, endive, pak choi, dragon fruit, Sharon fruit, kumquat and so on. For example, find out how it is classified and where it originated, describe its taste and how it is used in food preparation, and finally see if you can get some recipes that make use of this ingredient. If you can source your chosen ingredient locally, you might want to develop your own recipe and actually produce the dish. Alternatively, you could make up a recipe card that could be used to encourage people to eat their 'five a day'.

3 Recent statistics show that the UK's consumption of sweet potato has risen to such an extent that we are eating more sweet potatoes than traditional potatoes. Investigate the Irish Potato Famine (1845). Use your findings to discuss the importance of the potato as a staple food in Ireland/the UK.

4 Design a set of five questions that you can use to interview a group of people about their diet/understanding of the Eatwell plate. Collate and present your findings. What conclusions can you draw from your responses?

MORE ACTIVITIES FOR 'FUNCTIONAL PROPERTIES OF FOOD 2' (pp 40-41)

1 Investigate the coagulation of eggs when boiled for varying lengths of time. Use the table to record your results.

Length of time (mins)	Description
1	
3	
7	
10	

2 Investigate the shortening properties of fat.

Make pastry samples:

(a) Control recipe: 25g margarine to 50g plain flour

(b) 25g butter + 15g lard to 50g plain flour

(c) 25g margarine to 75g plain flour

(d) 25ml vegetable oil to 50g plain flour.

3 Produce the pastry via rubbing in, adding sufficient water to form a pastry. Roll, cut out and bake. Taste the samples. Reflect on the differences in taste and texture.

4 Investigate the denaturation of egg-whites by whisking them with an electric whisk for varying lengths of time. Use the table to record your results.

Length of time (mins)	Description
1	
3	
7	
10	

contd

5   Investigate the gluten content of flour:

Mix 50g of: (a) strong plain flour, (b) ordinary plain flour and (c) self-raising flour, separately with enough water to form a dough. Place each dough in a muslin square and rinse out the starch under a gentle stream of water. Squeeze the bag. Continue until no more starch is washed out and a small ball of gluten is left. Weigh out the individual gluten samples and work out the percentage of gluten in the different flours. Explain why there are differences.

6   Eggs are a very versatile ingredient. Design and make a dish/range of dishes that illustrates the different functional properties of eggs. Take a photograph of your dish and label/describe the different functions you have managed to include.

MORE ACTIVITIES FOR 'STAGES OF FOOD PRODUCT DEVELOPMENT' (pp 42–43)

Look at the following design briefs, choose one or two of them, and – working alone or in a group – go through the stages described above to develop your product for a specific market:

1   Design and make a new type of sandwich for a lacto-vegetarian.

2   Design and make a pasta dish which would appeal to children.

EXAMPLE OF AN 'IDENTIFY' AND 'GIVE REASONS FOR YOUR CHOICE' QUESTION (p 87)

EXAMPLE

A consumer wants to buy some beefburgers for a barbecue they are holding for 10 invited guests on 25 July.

Features	A ✔	B	C
Pack size	Pack of 20	Pack of 12	Pack of 8 ✘ not enough for people attending barbecue
Beef content	100% British beef	85% beef, 15% pork	80% beef
Shelf life	Best before 27 July	Best before 25 July	Best before 26 July
Cost	££	£££ ✘ most expensive	££

Key: £ Inexpensive   £££ Expensive

You will get a mark for identifying the most suitable beefburger for the consumer – in this case beefburger A. To reach this answer, it is a good idea for you to highlight the points of information in the table that help to lead you to this conclusion.

Examples of suitable reasons for choice in this case include:

• 'A' has a pack size of 20, which is suitable for the number of people attending the barbecue, giving them at least one each, and the option of a second one if they wish

• Beef content is 100% British beef, so the guests can be confident they will be eating a quality product

• Shelf life – best before 27 July means that any burgers left over will be able to be kept for a few more days and/or could be frozen for future use.

To answer this type of question, you must (1) pick a point of information from the table and then (2) offer a relevant reason linked to the scenario as to why it is the most suitable choice.

GLOSSARY

Additives
substances added to food to give different qualities, e.g. preservatives or colourings.

Aeration
process by which air is added, e.g. whisking egg-white traps air bubbles.

Allergies
unpleasant reactions to food experienced by some people.

Allotment
small area of land rented in order to grow one's own food.

Amino acids
the building blocks of protein. Children require 10 essential amino acids for growth, repair and maintenance of cells and tissues.

Anaemia
a condition where the amount of haemoglobin in the blood is below the normal level, or where there are fewer red blood cells than normal.

Anti-oxidants
the vitamins A, C and E, which help to destroy free radicals, thus preventing heart disease/some cancers. They also prevent rancidity in fats.

Attitudinal descriptions
beliefs about a food product, e.g. healthy, traditional.

Bacteria
a group of micro-organisms, some of which can cause food spoilage/food poisoning.

Binding agent
an ingredient that holds all the other ingredients together in a product, for example egg.

Biodegradable
able to be broken down by biological activity and to return into the environment.

Body Mass Index
a measure of body fat based upon height and weight.

Caramelisation
when sugar is heated, it melts and a caramel is formed.

Carbon footprint
for food, the total amount of CO_2 and other greenhouse gases emitted over the life cycle of a product.

Cholesterol
a fatty substance produced by the body; deposits may form, causing heart disease. Also found in some foods.

Closed questions
allow for quick responses that are easily analysed; also far easier for respondents to answer.

Coagulation
on the application of heat, proteins first denature and then set (e.g. when an egg cooks, the albumen changes from opaque to white). Once protein has coagulated, the changes are irreversible.

Collagen
a protein found in meat.

Concept generation
initial stage in product development where new ideas are thought up.

Concept screening
stage in product development where all ideas are filtered. Some ideas are rejected, others are taken forward.

Cross-contamination
the transfer of bacteria from one place to another – possibly resulting in food contamination.

Crystallisation
when sugar and water are boiled, the water is driven off and a thick syrup is formed. This sets on cooling, i.e. reverts to its crystal form.

Denaturation
a process where proteins lose their structure when heated.

Dental caries
tooth decay, i.e. when acids in your mouth dissolve the outer layers of your teeth.

Design brief
a situation/statement that outlines guidelines for the development task.

Dextrinisation
when starch is subjected to dry heat, a chemical change takes place: the starch molecules break down into dextrin. Dextrins are starch chains made up of glucose molecules.

Dietary Reference Values (DRVs)
the values for healthy groups of people which describe the range of desirable levels of consumption of a particular nutrient in a specific group of the population.

Disaccharides
created when two monosaccharides join together e.g. sucrose.

Disassembly
the process of taking something apart and looking at the individual parts.

Discrimination test
a sensory test aiming to evaluate specific attributes of a product. Objective test, i.e. not influenced by personal feelings.

Emulsification
the property that allows fats and oils to mix with water, preventing them from separating out. Lecithin, found in egg yolk, is a natural emulsifier.

Essential fatty acids
refer to Omega 3 and Omega 6 - known as essential because the body needs them, but cannot manufacture them itself. Associated with reducing cardiovascular disease.

Estimated Average Requirements (EARs)
the amount of nutrients most people need.

Factory farming

the process of raising a large number of livestock in confined conditions.

Fairtrade

ensures that disadvantaged farmers and workers in poor, developing countries get a better deal through the use of the international FAIRTRADE mark. Businesses work directly with suppliers to ensure that the workers are treated well and are given a fair, living wage for the products they produce.

Fermentation

the process of using yeast to convert sugar to carbon dioxide and alcohol. Used in the making of bread.

Foam

as eggs are whisked, air bubbles are beaten into the liquid, and the protein in egg denatures, making the mixture more stable. Egg-white alone can trap up to seven times its own volume in air, creating a foam.

Focus group

up to ten people who are asked interview questions about their perceptions, opinions and attitudes towards a product or concept.

Food Aid

provides food to groups of people who are in danger of starvation.

Food co-operatives

groups run by the community for the community, with the aim of supplying produce at non-profit-making affordable prices.

Food miles

the distance that food travels from where it is grown to where it is bought – sometimes referred to as 'from field to plate'. This is an environmental concern to some consumers because of the CO_2 emissions from transport.

Fortification

the addition of vitamins and minerals into foods in order to increase their nutritional value or to replace nutrients lost during processing.

Gelatinisation

on the application of heat, starch grains absorb water, then swell and burst, forming a gel.

Genetically Modified (GM)

plants or animals whose DNA has been altered to add extra nutrients or to make them more resistant to drought or insects.

Glazing

brushing beaten egg on top of a scone (etc.) before cooking, to achieve a shiny brown top.

Glucose

a simple sugar.

Gluten

the protein found in flour.

Halal

refers to food that has been prepared according to strict Islamic principles.

Hedonic descriptions

describe likes and dislikes, e.g. tasty, unpleasant.

High Biological Value (HBV) protein

a protein food which contains all of the essential amino acids in adequate amounts.

Hypertension

high blood pressure.

In season/seasonality

refers to the time of year that a food grows locally, e.g. Scottish raspberries are usually available from the end of June until September.

Intrinsic sugars

sugars contained in fruit, vegetables and milk.

Kosher

food that is prepared and eaten according to Jewish dietary laws.

Lactose

sugar found in milk.

Lipids

small molecules. Fats are lipids that are solid at room temperature; oils are lipids that are liquid at room temperature.

Macro nutrients

nutrients required in larger amounts by the body, i.e. protein, fat and carbohydrate.

Maillard browning

a chemical reaction that occurs between amino acids and sugar, usually resulting in a change of colour to dark brown.

Market research

gathering information that is used by manufacturers as part of the product-development process.

Marketing plan

how to promote a product to the target market. Four factors to consider: Product, Price, Place, Promotion.

Micro nutrients

nutrients needed in very small amounts by the body but still essential to maintain health, i.e. vitamins and minerals.

Modified-Atmosphere Packaging (MAP)

a method of preservation that involves changing the gases in the packaging in order to increase the shelf life of the food.

Monosaccharides

simplest form of sugar e.g. glucose, fructose.

Mycoprotein

a type of food, suitable for vegetarians, that is made by fermenting and harvesting fungus.

GLOSSARY

Non-milk extrinsic sugars
these are found in table sugar, honey and syrup, and in sweets and cakes.

Open questions
designed to give more depth and insight with responses to 'Why? How? What?' questions.

Organic
produced without the use of pesticides or chemical fertilisers.

Organoleptic factors
relate to aspects of food that are experienced by the senses: taste, sight, smell, touch.

Paired comparison test
a preference test where tasters are asked to taste two different samples and to say which dish (or characteristic) they prefer.

Palatability
describes the extent to which people find particular foods pleasing.

Pesticides
chemicals that are used to kill insects that could spoil farmers' crops.

Polysaccharides
many monosaccharides joined together e.g. starch.

Preference tests
subjective sensory tests to supply information about people's likes and dislikes of a product.

Preservation
preventing the growth of bacteria, fungi and micro-organisms; prolongs the life of a food.

Primary research
collecting original data through activities such as conducting interviews or getting people to complete a questionnaire.

Product launch
the point at which the new product is now on sale.

Product testing
when the product prototype(s) are tested on consumers so that their opinions can be gathered.

Profiling test
allows the intensity of the sensory characteristic to be tasted and recorded – usually on a star chart or diagram.

Prototype
a sample of what the developed product will look like.

Qualitative research
asking small groups of people for their opinions on products.

Quantitative research
surveying large numbers of people by questionnaires and interviews to obtain statistical data.

Ranking test
tasters are asked to rank products, or specific characteristics of products, in relation to how much or how little they like them.

Rating test
products, or specific characteristics of products, are tasted and then scored using a scale from 'like very much' to 'dislike very much'.

Satiety
when the body feels full after eating.

Secondary research
uses the primary research of others, typically in the form of research publications and reports. Secondary sources could include previous research reports, newspaper, magazine and journal content, and government statistics.

Sensory descriptions
describe texture, taste, smell or appearance of food, e.g. greasy, fruity, shiny.

Sensory evaluation
the process of using the senses to evaluate food samples in a controlled environment, and to record the results.

Shortening
refers to how 'short' or crumbly the texture of a product is.

Star diagram
a method of recording consumers' views about a product they have tasted, e.g. appearance, texture, aroma, taste.

Sustainability
using a process in food production that can be maintained for a long time.

Textured Vegetable Protein (TVP)
a food product, suitable for vegetarians and vegans, made from soya flour.

Triangle test
a discrimination test where tasters are given three samples (two the same and one different) and asked to identify the odd one out.

Umami
a Japanese term referring to a savoury taste.

Unique selling point
a marketing concept that aims to show something about the product to make it stand out to consumers and set it apart from the competition.

Vegan
a person who, through personal choice/belief, does not eat/use any product derived from animal origin.

Vegetarian
a person who abstains from the consumption of meat and meat products. Lacto-vegetarians will eat dairy produce; and ovo-lacto-vegetarians will also eat eggs.